THE POWER OF AFFIRMATIVE FAITH

Joyce —

You faith inspires + fills me deeply. When I saw this book, I thought of the Power you bring in your ministry to so many! Thank you for sharing your faith!

Blessings — Elizabeth

THE POWER OF AFFIRMATIVE FAITH

BRUCE G. EPPERLY

Chalice Press®
St. Louis, Missouri

Bible quotations, unless otherwise noted, are from the *New Revised Standard Version Bible,* copyright 1989, Division of Christian Education of the National Council of the Churches of Christ in the United States of America. Used by permission. All rights reserved.

Cover design: John Grizzell
Cover photograph: ©PhotoDisc
Interior design: Elizabeth Wright
Art direction: Michael Domínguez

This book is printed on acid-free, recycled paper.

Visit Chalice Press on the World Wide Web at
www.chalicepress.com

10 9 8 7 6 5 4 3 2 1   01 02 03 04 05 06

Library of Congress Cataloging–in–Publication Data

Epperly, Bruce Gordon.
　　The power of affirmative faith / by Bruce G. Epperly.
　　　　p.　　cm.
　　Includes bibliographical references and index.
　　ISBN 0-8272-2968-2
　　1. Spiritual life—Christianity　2. Affirmations.　　I. Title.
　　BV4501.2　　.E63　　2001
　　　248.4—dc21

　　　　　　　　　　　　　　　　　　　　　　　　　　　00-010284

Printed in the United States of America

Contents

Preface

This book is the result of my commitment for the past two decades to unite vital theology and holistic spirituality in the lives of laity, ministers, and seminary students. Today, I see a deep hunger within mainline and liberal churches for both a lively, life-orienting theology and a dynamic, life-transforming spirituality. I have written this book in order to provide the well-grounded spiritual nurture desperately needed in our time.

Last summer during a seminar at the Claremont School of Theology, I was asked to describe what is unique about process-relational Christian spirituality. The question inspired me to describe on paper the daily process of spiritual affirmations and practices that have motivated my own spiritual disciplines and my spiritual guidance of individuals and groups for nearly twenty years. I believe that the dynamic, relational, and incarnational worldview affirmed by process theology can inspire both personal and spiritual transformation. I also believe that process theology's affirmation of God's creative presence in every moment of life enables persons to experience the divine aim at beauty, transformation, and reconciliation in every encounter. Indeed, process spirituality's understanding of God's presence throughout history in human experience has made the biblical image of an intimate, personal, and adventurous God come alive for me and many others. We have encountered a living Christ who invites us to open our hearts to the profound ethnic and spiritual pluralism of our time.

Although process philosophy and theology was initially articulated by philosophers such as Alfred North Whitehead and Charles Hartshorne and theologians such as Bernard Loomer and John Cobb, I believe that process spirituality is a deeply biblical spirituality that reminds us that we are always walking on "holy ground" in companionship with the Holy Adventurer. Indeed, process theology and spirituality are significant precisely because they enable persons and communities to experience Christ in an intimate and transformative way.

The Power of Affirmative Faith is an invitation to a dynamic, contemporary spiritual discipline, embracing tradition and novelty, scripture and spirituality, personal growth and social change, body and spirit, meditation and dance, liturgy and play, individuality and relationship. Deeply theological, this process is also intensely practical.

This holistic process of spiritual formation brings transformation to every aspect of life, including physical well-being. This book is my gift to those twenty-first-century spiritual seekers whose goal is to experience God's lively and surprising presence "on earth as it is in heaven."

In the spirit of Paul's image of the body of Christ, I would like to express my gratitude to the communion of saints whose inspiration and love have brought this book into existence.

While these saints are too numerous to name, it is important to me to give thanks to certain "named" saints. Martha van Hoy's quest for a lively, open-spirited daily devotional book was the initial inspiration behind this book. This book was written for Martha and countless other persons who seek a spiritual path congruent with an inclusive, incarnational theology.

For more than twenty-five years, Professor John B. Cobb of the Claremont School of Theology has been my theological mentor and the embodiment of the creative synthesis of theological reflection and care for the Earth as a whole, as well as care for the struggles of individual students. Rev. Patricia Adams Farmer's encouragement and belief in the importance of my work for the church today has been a constant inspiration. My brother, Bill Epperly, and father, Everett Epperly, have been examples of what it means to face the abyss of chronic illness and anxiety with ordinary, yet exceptional, day-to-day courage. My son, Matt Epperly, has inspired me to embody the virtues of integrity, imagination, and innovation in my parenting and personal life. My wife, Rev. Kate Epperly, has lovingly challenged me to achieve excellence as a pastor, professor, writer, and spiritual director. Throughout the whole process, I am thankful for God's moment-by-moment inspiration that has enabled me to experience the totality of my life within the horizon of God's surprising and adventurous love.

Potomac, Maryland
New Year's Day 2000

Acknowledgments

"Come and Find the Quiet Center." Text: Shirley Erena Murray. © 1992 Hope Publishing Co., Carol Stream, IL 60188. All rights reserved. Used by permission.

"Creator God, Creating Still." Words © 1977 from *A Singing Faith* by Jane Parker Huber, Westminster Press, 1987. Used by permission.

Excerpt from "For the Time Being." From *W. H. Auden Collected Poems* by W. H. Auden. Copyright © 1944 & renewed 1972 by W. H. Auden. Reprinted by permission of Random House, Inc.

"Here I Am, Lord." © 1981, Daniel L. Schutte and New Dawn Music, 5536 NE Hassalo, Portland, OR 97213. All rights reserved. Used with permission.

"Holy and Good Is the Gift of Desire." By Thomas H. Troeger, from *Borrowed Light*, © 1994 Oxford University Press, Inc. Used by permission. All rights reserved.

"I Am the Light of the World." Words & Music by Strathdee. Copyright © 1969 by Desert Flower Music, P. O. Box 1476, Carmichael, CA 95609. Used by permission.

The lines from "i thank You God for most this amazing." Copyright 1950, © 1978, 1991 by the Trustees for the E.E. Cummings Trust. Copyright© 1979 by George James Firmage, from *Complete Poems: 1904–1962* by E.E. Cummings, edited by George J. Firmage. Used by permission of Liveright Publishing Corporation.

"I Was There to Hear Your Borning Cry." Used by permission. © 1985 John Ylvisaker, Box 321, Waverly, Iowa 50577.

"Let Hope and Sorrow Now Unite." Text: Brian Wren. © 1983 Hope Publishing Co., Carol Stream, IL 60188. All rights reserved. Used by permission.

CHAPTER ONE

Transforming Your Mind

*Do not be conformed to this world, but be transformed by
the renewing of your minds, so that you may discern what
is the will of God—what is good and acceptable and
perfect.*

ROMANS 12:2

In the spring of 1999, my seventeen-year position as senior Protestant chaplain and director of the Protestant ministry at Georgetown University was eliminated due to university "downsizing." In a moment's conversation with my supervisor, a career that involved seventeen years of innovative and expanding ministry was ended. The ministry I had founded and the programs I had initiated would now be under the direction of part-time chaplains.

The termination of my ministry was unexpected and poorly handled by the university administration. Although student and faculty protests were held throughout the campus, the university administration stood firmly by its decision to terminate the position. Initially, the decision defied my sense of reality and justice. Like one who has just lost a spouse or parent, I had to remind myself for the first few weeks that this was reality and not just a bad dream from which I would eventually awaken! My innovative ecumenical work in campus ministry had been

1

nationally acclaimed. I was respected on Georgetown's campus as a scholar, teacher, pastor, and spiritual guide and had recently won a number of prestigious academic awards. I believed that the excellence and innovation that had characterized my work would ensure job security, regardless of the university's financial constraints. I truly believed that this job would be mine until my retirement, should I so desire. I had spent the majority of my adult life as a university chaplain at Georgetown University. Now, at age forty-six, I would be starting all over! *How could this be happening to me? What did I do to deserve such treatment at this time of my life?* I asked myself.

When my initial shock and denial subsided, I realized that the termination of my position had plunged me into a spiritual as well as vocational crisis. As the Chinese characters for the word *crisis* suggest, both danger and opportunity lay before me as I looked toward an uncertain future. I felt as if I were reliving my father's history. Almost forty years earlier, my father—at age fifty-three—lost his position as pastor of Community Baptist Church in King City, California. He never fully recovered emotionally or professionally from this midlife vocational crisis. Now, in my midlife, I would have to face the same challenges that defeated my father. Deep in my heart, I knew that only two options lay before me—either choose life and see the termination of this ministry as the unexpected invitation to a new and surprising adventure or choose death and see the university's decision as a sign of my own personal impotence. Even though I did not have a positive parental model for facing such dramatic change, I decided to choose life and look for the adventure amid the chaos of midlife job transition and vocational insecurity. With God's guidance, I trusted that I would find a new personal adventure for the years ahead.

As a university chaplain, professor, author, and lecturer on spirituality, health, and wholeness, I also knew that I was being put to a personal test. In the past, I had counseled many persons who suddenly found themselves the victims of downsizing and other unexpected life changes. Now, I would have to listen to my own counsel and the wisdom of my own Christian faith tradition. Although I did not believe that God had chosen the events that led to the termination of my position, I *did* believe that with these upheavals God was leading me toward new horizons in my vocational and spiritual lives. Still, as I faced the uncharted horizons of my vocational future, would I practice what I had preached? Would I act as if God did not exist and I had no personal resources to face this difficult time? Or would I trust that God's presence would sustain, empower, and energize me with new ideas and creative solutions even in the midst of insecurity? Would I open myself to God's moment-by-moment guidance or simply trust my own constricted and fearful judgment?

Although the wounds of grief and the passions of anger ran deep in my heart for several weeks, I came to believe that only one path lay before me if I were to honor my vocation and faith in the risen Lord. I committed myself to choosing, one moment at a time, the new possibilities that God would be offering me. Despite my fears, I decided to press onward with the faith that God was truly guiding my life toward a new horizon of adventure. I knew that choosing life would be a difficult and day-to-day challenge, given the deep memories of my father's passivity and lingering depression and my own personal feelings of insecurity and betrayal. But I also knew that in the crucible of this challenge, I would experience renewed faith and a deeper sense of divine grace and empowerment. This book of affirmations reflects my commitment to live by the spirit of creative transformation and holy adventure in a time of uncertainty. But more important, it also reflects the unexpected and surprising presence of God in every life situation.

I know that my story is far from unusual. As the earthquake-wise California bumper sticker notes, "Shift happens!" If you haven't had it happen to you, it has happened to someone you know and love. But I suspect that it may be your story as well. At some point in our lives, most of us will experience the rumblings of a spiritual, emotional, relational, or vocational earthquake, the force of which will shake the very foundations of our lives. If nothing else, we will face the death or serious illness of someone or something we love. As C. S. Lewis notes in his classic text on bereavement, *A Grief Observed,* death and grief are as essential to a good marriage as courtship and engagement. Even the traditional marriage vows note the reality of loss with the words "till death do us part." One way or the other, when our familiar world collapses, the words of Psalm 46 become our own personal story:

> The earth should change…
>> the mountains shake in the heart of the sea…
> its waters roar and foam…
>> the mountains tremble with its tumult.

At such moments, we search for a firm foundation for our lives, a reality that is sure and dependable amid the tumult of change and the chaos of uncertainty. Life is change. The birds of the air and the lilies of the field pass away with tomorrow's sunrise. We experience the constancy of change—embracing and letting go—as we observe our own aging process and see the transformation of our children from infants to adults in what seems like a blink of an eye. We anxiously await the changes that may result from our company's merger with a larger corporation, the resignation of a beloved spiritual leader, or the impending separation and divorce that will mean much more than a new address and a new set of parental responsibilities. At such times of dislocation and uncertainty, we pray that we can embody the psalmist's own hard-won affirmation of faith:

> God is our refuge and strength,
>> a very present help in trouble.
> Therefore we will not fear, though the earth should change,
>> though the mountains shake in the heart of the sea...
> The LORD of hosts is with us;
>> the God of Jacob is our refuge...
> "Be still, and know that I am God!
>> I am exalted among the nations,
>> I am exalted in the earth."
> The LORD of hosts is with us;
>> the God of Jacob is our refuge. (Ps. 46:1–2, 7, 10–11)

When my professional world collapsed, I had to choose between life and death, love and fear, abundance and scarcity. I had to trust the affirmations of faith I had repeated over the years. I had to claim, more powerfully than ever before, that God was intimately involved in my life and that God would continue to be my refuge and strength. During this time of transition, I have been consoled and empowered each day by the living affirmations of faith from scripture and the Christian theological and spiritual tradition. I have been sustained on a daily basis by divine promises, such as "[Nothing] will be able to separate us from the love of God in Christ Jesus our Lord" (Rom. 8:38–39); "All things work together for good" (Rom. 8:28); and "I came that they may have life, and have it abundantly" (Jn. 10:10).

As I looked toward the immediate future following the termination of my position, I realized how easy it would be for me to live by scarcity, isolation, and fear. With God's dynamic possibilities all around me, I might be tempted to live as if everything depended on my own meager and ineffectual efforts. I might forget the divine companionship that had sustained, challenged, and empowered me through the years. In the first few weeks, I often felt like the woman who saved for many years for a sea cruise. At each mealtime during the cruise, she stayed in her cabin eating peanut butter and jelly sandwiches while her neighbors dined on filet mignon and crepes. When one of her fellow passengers asked why he hadn't seen her at dinner, she replied—much to his amazement—that she was saving her money for the final dinner on board. She had not realized that her meals were included in her fare! A place at the bountiful table had always been set for her, but she had missed it by living within her own perceptions of scarcity.

It has been said that there are really only two kinds of persons in the world: those who are in God's hands and know it, and those who are in God's hands and don't! Today, medical researchers are realizing that our beliefs and interpretations of reality can actually cure or kill us. What we believe about ourselves and God can be a matter of life and death, whether we are seeking employment or living with a life-threatening illness. As we face the challenges of life, will we live by divine abundance or individualistic scarcity?

Stricken with lung cancer, David gave up all hope. A lifetime smoker, he initially asserted that he deserved to die and that cancer was God's way of punishing him. He believed, in the wake of his diagnosis, that all he could do now was wait for the inevitability of the death he felt he deserved. David was surprised when his physician told him that as a result of early detection, his chances of survival from a medical perspective were relatively good. But he was also warned that the path toward a cure would be an arduous journey involving surgery and chemotherapy. As he faced the future, David realized that if he were to survive, he would have to choose life. He would have to go to work—medically, emotionally, and spiritually. Thumbing through his Bible in search of guidance, he came upon a verse that transformed his life: "While we still were sinners Christ died for us" (Rom. 5:8). Waves of grace flowed through him over the next few weeks. He realized that he didn't have to be perfect in order to be forgiven. As he read about the healings of Jesus, David discovered that God was not punishing him with cancer. God wanted him to live and make a new beginning as a spouse, parent, and friend. From that point on, he decided that he would choose life and live by the simple affirmation of God's intimate love for him. Whenever he felt unworthy, he prayerfully returned to those saving words that became his shield and protection: While I was a sinner Christ died for me! God loves me! Today, David is cancer-free. He knows that his physical well-being and spiritual wholeness are the result of both good medical care and a transformed mind.

A member of a fundamentalist Christian sect, Susan believed that taking her children to see a doctor when they were ill was a sign of faithlessness. When her daughter had severe stomach pains, she refused to take her to the hospital. Instead, she gathered fellow believers around her for a prayer circle. Two days later her daughter died of appendicitis, even though the emergency room was only two blocks away. Our spiritual beliefs have consequences: Beliefs issue into actions; theology becomes biology; and our faith can cure or kill!

When Martha was diagnosed with breast cancer, she took a long hard look at her life. Despite her financial and professional successes, what she saw as she looked in the mirror of her life was a woman dominated by low self-esteem, shame, and passivity. In her competitive profession, she felt the constant need to prove herself and stay ahead of the pack. Always on the alert, she devoted little time to personal renewal and spiritual growth. Faced with a life-shattering medical diagnosis, she knew that breast cancer could herald either the end of life or the beginning of a new one. Following her physician's guidance, she chose a lumpectomy and a regimen of chemotherapy, but she also chose to renew her mind and transform her spirit.

Since her mother's death of breast cancer, Martha had been a marginal Christian. Although she no longer claimed the Calvinistic theology of her childhood church, she believed deep down that God had willed her mother's cancer and that breast cancer would eventually be her own tragic destiny. As she reviewed her life story, Martha recognized that the quality of her future spiritual life could be a matter of life and death. She embarked on a journey that included pastoral counseling, spiritual guidance, visualization, meditation, dietary changes, complementary medicine, and prayer. She began to visualize God's light surrounding and permeating her breasts. She also began using affirmations of faith, such as "God's light shines in me, healing every cell of my body" and "nothing can separate me from the love of God," several times each day. She began to reimagine her breasts in terms of their beauty and life-giving function rather than as malignant hazards to her health. She realized that God did not intend for her to relive her mother's passive response to the diagnosis of cancer. God intended her to have abundant life, whether that meant one year or fifty years.

Even in the midst of her health crisis, Martha began to live by God's abundance: She reached out to new friends, took up painting, and began to date a man she met in a spiritual growth group at her church. Today, Martha is cancer-free, married, and the mother of a healthy, breast-feeding baby. She has found a creative way to achieve excellence in parenting and marriage as well as in her profession. She is thankful for the medical technology that cured her disease, but she is equally thankful for the spiritual transformation that healed her life. Even if the cancer returns, Martha's mind has been transformed, and she is a new creation.

She believes deeply that her life is in the hands of a loving, creative, and empowering God.

I believe that humankind is on the verge of a profound spiritual transformation that will change the way we look at health and medicine, human potential, and planetary survival. I have found an invitation to spiritual transformation emerging in the lively, pluralistic world of the twenty-first century that is grounded in the ancient wisdom of the sages of East and West as well as the philosophical speculations of the new physics. Put simply, this spiritual wisdom proclaims that *you* are a child of God, infinite in worth, connected deeply with the dynamic spirit of God, and creative and powerful beyond your imagination. This wisdom proclaims that God is intimately involved in our lives, bringing forth new and surprising possibilities. In partnership with the divinity present in all things, you can change your life and change the world! While we are not the omnipotent masters of fate, we are also not impotent bystanders in our own lives. We are meant to be partners with God in the creation of a beautiful world. Our lives and deaths are in God's hands, and God will supply our needs even in the darkest situations. Moving from scarcity to abundance and from fear to love is the gift of the God who calls us to live by these affirmations every day of our lives. By using spiritual affirmations, visualizations, and creative actions, we can experience renewed and transformed minds that enable us to see who we truly are and to find wholeness in every life situation.

While the power of affirmative faith is recognized throughout the biblical tradition, Paul's counsel to the church at Rome is the touchstone for the creative transformation of our minds, bodies, relationships, and communities: "Do not be conformed to this world, but be transformed by the renewing of your minds, so that you may discern what is the will of God—what is good and acceptable and perfect" (Rom. 12:2). Paul's words capture the essence of what biblical scholar Walter Brueggemann has described as the "prophetic imagination," the courage to live by an alternative reality rather than by the unjust and confining structures of the world and our personal existence.

Faith involves an alternative vision of ourselves and the world. Faith involves intellectually affirming—and then living and embodying the affirmation—that this is God's world and that we are all God's children, heirs to an infinite creativity and power. Martin Luther once spoke of faith as a "lively, reckless confidence in the grace of God." I would expand on Luther's words to read, "Faith is lively openness to the constant transformative power of God's grace." When we change our minds and our interpretations of reality, everything in our lives is transformed. We become conscious members of the body of Christ. We discover that we have abundant personal and relational resources, even when our finances are modest. Death and scarcity no longer rule our politics or our personal lives. We envisage a world where all life is connected and supported by God's loving care and where the success of one person adds to the success of everyone else. Zero-sum, bottom-line thinking gives way to the unlimited horizons of abundant life.

To the person who lives by faith's affirmations, the world is an open system in which new energies are constantly flowing from the inexhaustible resources of a loving God. From the perspective of an affirmative faith, God will truly supply all our needs. Indeed, God is already supplying our deepest needs even when we are unaware of it!

A transformed mind can be a matter of life and death. In his classic account of the Holocaust, *Man's Search for Meaning,* Victor Frankl demonstrates the survival value of the transformed mind. Frankl attributes his own survival in the Nazi concentration camps to his commitment to complete his work in psychology and his hope to be reunited with his wife after the war. In looking beyond the barbed wire and the crematoria, Frankl placed his suffering in a larger perspective. Although evil and indignity were everyday realities at the camps, the Nazi atrocities did not fully define Frankl's experience or place limits on his dreams. Looking back on the Holocaust, Frankl affirms the life-changing power of an "attitudinal heroism" grounded in a person's decision to claim the right to choose her or his attitude toward life even when all other choices have been denied. According to Frankl,

> The experiences of camp life show that man does have a choice of action. There were enough examples, often of a heroic nature, which proved that apathy can be overcome, irritability suppressed. [A human] *can* preserve a vestige of spiritual freedom, of independence of mind, even in such terrible conditions of psychic and physical duress.[1]

Frankl maintains that even the experience of suffering and injustice can be a factor in personal transformation for those persons who commit themselves to the ongoing search for meaning. "It is just such an exceptionally difficult external situation which gives one the opportunity to grow spiritually beyond himself."[2] Those prisoners who failed to recognize their inner resources found their lives meaningless and their health at risk. "The prisoner who had lost faith in the future—his future— was doomed. With his loss in belief in the future, he also lost his spiritual hold: he let himself decline and become subject to mental and physical decay."[3]

In words that anticipate the current interest in mind-body medicine, Frankl asserts, "Those who know how close a connection between the state of mind—his courage and hope, or lack of them—and the state of immunity of his body will understand that a sudden loss of courage and hope can have a deadly effect."[4] Belief eventually becomes biology. As medical studies indicate, hope in the future empowers the cardiovascular and immune systems and energizes our cells and organs.

The power of a personally lived affirmation is demonstrated in the award-winning film *Life is Beautiful*. Caught along with his wife and young son in the chaos and terror of a concentration camp, the father creates an alternative reality to the death and dehumanization of the concentration camp—an imaginative game in which his son's patience, courage, and ability to hide are rewarded. By utilizing the power of the imagination, the father creates a safe world of freedom and creativity that protects his son spiritually as well as physically from the insanity of the death camp. I believe that the film *Life is Beautiful* asks the provocative and life-transforming question: Which is more real—the concentration camp or the father's imagination? the Nazi cruelty or a father's love? The answer is clear to persons who live by their affirmations: There is a larger reality than the concentration camp—the world of imagination and possibility, the universe of divine care and resourcefulness. In saying yes to the world of the imagination, you are saying yes to life and to the lives of those you love, and you are saying yes to God's vision for your life. Although they often appear counterfactual, the affirmations of faith manifest a deeper reality than the unimaginative realism of everyday life.

Martin Luther King, Jr., once proclaimed, "I have a dream." The dreamer's vision of a transformed America reflected his own deep affirmations of faith. In his sermon "Our God Is Able," King relates his own experience of personal transformation. One evening during the most contentious days of the Montgomery bus boycott, King received an anonymous phone call that threatened the lives of his family and himself. Trembling with fear and unable to sleep, King went downstairs for a cup of coffee. As the coffee brewed, King bowed his head over the kitchen table and prayed aloud: "I am here taking a stand for what is right. But now I am afraid. The people are looking to me for leadership, and if I stand before them without strength or courage, they too will falter. I am at the end of my powers. I have nothing left. I have come to the point where I can't make it alone." In that moment, King experienced the presence of God in a way that would forever transform the way he looked at reality. King heard the quiet, yet powerful assurance of an inner voice saying, "Stand up for righteousness, stand up for truth. God will be at your side forever." In King's own words, "My uncertainty disappeared. I was ready to face anything. The outer situation remained the same, but God had given me inner calm." Although he faced beatings, bombings, imprisonment, and threats, King could still affirm, in the midst of conflict, "God is able to give us the inner resources to face the storms and problems of life."[5] Imprisoned in the Birmingham jail a few years later, King's spirit could not be confined as he wrote one of the masterpieces of twentieth-century social ethics, "Letter from the Birmingham Jail," on scraps of paper supplied by a jail trustee. Once again, look at King's affirmation. Repeat it daily, if you are currently facing one of life's storms: "God is able to give us the inner resources to face the storms and problems of life."

The transformed mind can change history, and it can also change the life of a family. A number of years ago my marriage had reached a crisis point. A pastoral counselor had pronounced our marriage dead, and we had begun to believe her. Still, in spite of our fear and alienation, we decided to give our marriage one more chance. My wife and I still cared for each other, and we desired deeply that our young son Matthew have a secure and loving home. Uncertain of the future, we decided to take our faith in God's power seriously. As students of the psychiatrist Jerry Jampolsky, noted for his work in "attitudinal healing" in children diagnosed with cancer, we chose to treat our relationship as if it were being threatened by a potentially deadly disease. We gave ourselves one year to transform our marriage. We chose to live only by our affirmations of ourselves and each other. We chose to speak words of support and care and to minimize even constructive criticism. Like the sculptor Michelangelo, we chose to see the angels within the boulders of each other and opportunities for growth in the difficulties of our relationship. To our own and our therapist's surprise, our relationship was healed and transformed. We renewed our marriage vows in the summer of 1989. The transformation of our marriage was not the result of denying our marital conflicts or personal imperfections or an unhealthy codependence, but a willingness to see the holy and beautiful in each other, to claim our spiritual responsibilities as parents, and to see the negative aspects of our relationship within a wider perspective of respect, partnership, and love. Although our marriage is still not, and will never be, perfect, today it is as strong as an oak tree, and it gives support to other couples around us. We discovered that a healthy marriage is founded on living by the affirmations of our faith: the recognition of God's image in each other, the willingness to constantly live by forgiveness, and the commitment to see our marriage as a witness to God's love and a partnership in serving humankind. By living by our affirmations of faith, we came to see our marriage from a larger perspective as part of God's own invitation to partnership in and cocreation of a world of healing, wholeness, reconciliation, and justice. We discovered that a healthy and growing marriage is as much a result of our interpretation of reality and each other as the initial attractions of beauty and mutual interests.

At the heart of any faith tradition is a constellation of affirmations that shape the believers' actions and interpretations of reality. These affirmations about the nature of reality are found in the traditional ecumenical creeds of the church as well as the modern statements of faith formulated by denominations such as the Christian Church (Disciples of Christ), the United Church of Christ, and the United Church of Canada. These affirmations shape our experiences and hopes as Christians. Although we are called in this pluralistic age to recognize and affirm divine truth wherever it is found, whether in Buddhism, Islam, or Judaism, it is clear that each tradition interprets reality from a different perspective. Although the affirmations of faith of the various religious traditions are dynamic and evolving and are being transformed as a result of interfaith dialogue and the emerging interplay of spirituality and science, the uniquely Christian affirmations of faith revolve around a vision of God's presence in history, the nature of human existence, the relationship of spirituality and embodiment, and divine revelation that differ in content and emphasis from Buddhist, Islamic, or Hindu affirmations. As Christians, we see the world in light of God's healing and transforming presence in Jesus of Nazareth, the one we call the Christ. Because "believing is seeing," Christians experience different possibilities for spiritual growth than Buddhists, perhaps, do and often see different perspectives on the same experience. Difference in perspective does not mean relativism or religious imperialism; rather, it affirms the power of the mind to interpret, shape, and understand the realities that we experience, especially the encounter with the living God. Although we may look "into a glass darkly," the spectacles through which we perceive both the world and our lives are profoundly influenced by the Christian affirmations of faith in God's actions in history and in the life and teaching of Jesus the Savior. In short, we see the world through the eyes of Christ.

Although the traditional affirmations of faith have often been reduced to abstract doctrines, their true purpose is to reflect and shape our understanding of reality. Ultimately, doctrine and scripture arise from deep experiences of faith and encounters with the divine reality. Before the early Christians spoke of Jesus as the *Christ*, the Greek word for the Hebraic Messiah, they experienced his transforming their physical, spiritual, and relational lives. Before the apostle Paul became a theologian and evangelist of grace, he experienced the mystery of encountering the resurrected Christ and the surprising and graceful forgiveness of God.

To shape our lives authentically, the doctrines of faith must become living affirmations, concrete experiences and lenses through which we interpret our daily realities. To speak of God as "creator of heaven and earth," for example, involves making a statement about God's ongoing creativity and the nature of the created world—God is the reality behind the "big bang" and the creative guide of the evolutionary process; but it also involves an interpretation of our personal reality—the world and my life are, moment by moment, in God's hands, my life and the events in my life occur in the context of a dynamic and meaningful universe that supports my deepest needs and desires.

We live by what we affirm. Although our affirmations of faith may lead us to oppose certain individual and corporate behaviors as life-destructive, their primary purpose is to express our deep, faithful experiences of God and to edify the spiritual experiences of others by inviting persons to see God's presence at work in their own lives. This is a far cry from the divisive use of creeds and doctrines as weapons of spiritual warfare, theological hairsplitting, and ecclesiastical excommunication. When we forget that the primary purpose of affirmations of faith is to nurture spiritual wholeness and to edify the faith of ourselves and others, our doctrines become lifeless, divisive, and destructive.

Our affirmations shape our interpretations of reality and make firm our beliefs. They also give us a moral compass in our personal and ethical decision making. When Desmond Tutu spoke of Apartheid as a heresy, he was invoking the affirmation that humankind is created in the divine image and that, accordingly, all humans are of inherent value. When the Quaker John Woolman walked across America dressed in hopsack rather than indigo-dyed clothing acquired through slave trading, his protest against slavery was grounded in his perception of the inner light present in all humankind, including African slaves. When the soup kitchen volunteer nods to each person in the cafeteria line with a smile and a kind word, she affirms that "Someday Jesus may be coming down this line, and I want to treat him real good!" When a young adult chooses to become a diversity leader at her high school, her actions are grounded in her belief that God's artistry is reflected in the many-hued human adventure.

Our affirmations take flesh in everyday life. What we believe in—what we firmly hold as true for ourselves and the world—is revealed in our responses to conflicts at church and the office, our treatment of persons of other ethnic backgrounds, the stewardship of our resources, and our responses to devasting news. We become what we affirm, and we act out what we are becoming. Indeed, our affirmations of faith serve as antidotes to our personal and cultural experiences of fear, scarcity, and division.

Still, many of us feel halfhearted in trusting our affirmations and beliefs. With African American mystic/theologian/pastor Howard Thurman, we may intellectually believe the truths of faith, but the rest of us hasn't "caught up"—our stomachs and hearts also need to be convinced of God's care in times of crisis and conflict. Affirmations of faith help the rest of our being to "catch up" as they transform both our conscious and unconsious interpretations of reality. Our affirmations embrace the renewing of our minds but take shape in the movement of our bodies and the exploration of our imaginations.

As a Baptist child, I often bridled against my mother's desire that my brother and I should memorize a Bible verse each week. I instinctively chose the shortest verses, including the shortest of them all, "Jesus wept," for my weekly memorization. At the time, such memorization was just another burden, and my mother's rationale—you would have something to give you strength if you were ever put in prison following a Communist takeover of America—made little sense. Now I realize the importance of these heartfelt, deeply held, and firmly remembered words of faith. In times of indecision, moral temptation, and political conflict, they are the mantras, the repeated words of strength, that show us the way through the darkness and give us the power to live faithfully.

Just think of the words of affirmation that you have heard at the bedside or the graveside: A widow proclaims, "What gets me through these lonely days is my faith that God is with me and that my husband is in God's hands"; during a regimen of chemotherapy a young father repeats, "God's loving care is showing me a new way to live and giving me the strength to face the possibility of death"; or a middle-aged man, experiencing symptoms of a heart attack, calms his anxiety by repeating "Nothing can separate me from the love of God" as his wife drives him to the emergency room. In this same spirit, I recently advised a young woman beginning a course of chemotherapy to visualize the "light of Christ" entering her body along with the chemical infusion. Rather than being an "enemy" that will give her nausea and cause her hair to fall out, she now sees her chemotherapy treatments as a gift from God intended for her healing. While she images the healing light of God, she also repeats to herself, "God's healing light fills and surrounds my body. I am always in God's loving care."

In changing our "self-talk" from negativity to optimism—a secular description of the transformation that occurs when we begin to live by our affirmations of faith—we change our emotional responses and interpretations of the events of our lives, and we change our behaviors. Our affirmations of faith become for us the bread of life and living waters as they permeate our whole beings—waking and sleeping. When we are alive to our affirmations of faith, even the most tragic experiences reveal the presence of a loving and nurturing God, within whose care we "live, move, and have our being."

The power of faith to heal and transform our lives is now being documented by physicians and scientists as well as spiritual healers. According to Harold Koenig, director of Duke University's Center for the Study of Religion/Spirituality and Health, recent medical studies have indicated the significance of intrinsic, or deeply held, faith in the following areas:

(1) People who regularly attend church, pray individually, and read the Bible regularly have significantly lower blood pressure than those who are less religious.

(2) People who attend church regularly are hospitalized much less often than those who rarely attend church.

(3) People who have a deep religious faith are less likely to suffer depression from stressful life events and are more likely, if they do suffer depression, to recover than those who are less religious.

(4) The deeper a person's religious faith, the less likely he or she is to be overwhelmed by depression during or following a hospitalization for physical illness.

(5) Religious people have healthier lifestyles.

(6) Elders with a deep personal faith have a stronger sense of well-being and life satisfaction than less religious persons.

(7) People with strong faith who suffer from physical illnesses have significantly better outcomes than less religious people.

(8) Regular church participation is linked with a stronger immune system.

(9) Religious persons live longer and have statistically fewer diagnoses of heart disease and cancer.

(10) Deeply religious persons are better able to cope with bereavement and mortality than nonreligious persons.[6]

Although there are many reasons why religious persons and church participants live longer and have healthier lives on average than those for whom religion is peripheral—the importance of social support and connectedness to the wider community, the importance of physical touch, and the intensified presence of God in religious settings—I believe that at the heart of the "faith factor," as described by Georgetown University physician Dale Matthews, is the commitment of these persons to live by certain deeply held and life-transforming affirmations of faith.[7] Their affirmations of faith issue forth in church involvement, community service, and the endurance and redemption of suffering. The beliefs that have shaped their characters have become their biology, and their faith has made them whole.

Our affirmations of faith take many forms. They can be verbal, visual, written, chanted, sung, danced, or acted out. Regardless of the form, authentic and repeated focus on the love, protection, and creativity of God transforms the character, renews the mind, and enhances one's physical and emotional well-being. The following paragraphs point out the power of faith's affirmations to change our lives.

Herbert Benson has pointed out the benefits of the "relaxation response," the silent repetition of a word for fifteen to twenty minutes twice daily, in lowering blood pressure, improving immune system function, and reducing stress. Recently, Benson has suggested that we can go "beyond the relaxation response" by choosing to repeat not just any word but a meaningful word of faith (e.g., "God," "light," "peace") as the focus of meditation. Benson believes that the use of a meaningful word serves to enhance the benefits of meditation by combining the physiological benefits of the relaxation response with the placebo effect, the impact of our beliefs on our overall well-being, including our cardiovascular and immune systems. Long before Benson's discovery of meditative prayer, Christians practiced various forms of "centering prayers," such as the Rosary, the Jesus Prayer ("Lord, Jesus Christ, have mercy upon me a sinner"), and the prayer of the "cloud of unknowing" (the simple focus on a word such as "God," "love," or "Christ"). Today, the practice of "centering prayer," revived in a modern form by Basil Pennington and Thomas Keating, is taught at many churches. Through the repetition of a meaningful prayer word, the restless mind is calmed, and the intimate presence of God becomes a reality in the meditator's life. The repetition of these spiritual affirmations changes our attitudes as well as our physiology.

Other Christians such as United Church of Christ minister and mystic Alan Armstrong Hunter, one of my own spiritual guides, combine "breath prayers" with their affirmations. As they inhale, they may simply repeat, "I breathe the spirit deeply in." With every exhalation, they may choose simply to say, "and blow it thankfully out again," or let go of negativity with each breath with words such as, "and blow it out anxiously (or nervously, or angrily) again." This type of breath prayer has recently been popularized by the Buddhist monk Thich Nhat Hanh, whose approach involves repeating, "Breathing in I feel calm, breathing out I smile," as a means of experiencing peace in any situation.

The affirmations of faith can also be visual representations of our deepest beliefs. Before I preach a sermon or teach a class, I visualize the chapel, classroom, and participants as being surrounded by the divine light permeating all things. In the spirit of the Hindu word *namaste,* "the divine in me greets the divine in you," I seek to visualize Christ's presence in each new encounter. Following the guidance of Methodist minister and spiritual guide Maxie Dunnam, I often silently whisper, "I give Christ to you and receive Christ from you," as I see the divine light surrounding those I meet. This affirmation of God's presence in others has often enabled me to face conflict situations at work with a spirit of reconciliation.

Like Martha, whose spiritual practices were pivotal in her healing response to the diagnosis of breast cancer, many persons with cancer visualize the cancer cells being embraced, engulfed, and eliminated by the divine healing light. As I stated earlier, other persons undergoing treatments for cancer imagine their chemotherapy as a eucharistic sharing in the body and blood of Christ. In opening to the divine healing light, they discover that God's spacious presence, rather than the cancer, defines their self-understanding and personal experience. In so doing, they move from being victims to being cocreators with God in the healing adventures of their lives.

Episcopalian spiritual healer Agnes Sanford often invoked the power of visualization and imagination in her own healing ministry. In her spiritual care of a young boy with a leaky heart valve, Sanford asked the boy to play a pretend game with her.

Pretend you're a big boy going to high school and you're on the football squad. Shut your eyes and see yourself holding the ball and running ahead of all the other fellows. "Look at that guy," the other kids will say. "Just look at him run! Boy, he's strong! I bet he's got a strong heart!" Then you say, "Thank you, God, because that's the way it's going to be." Will you play that game every night, right after you say your going-to-bed prayers?[8]

At his next examination, the physician pronounced the boy well. Although visualized affirmations of faith are not a panacea or magic, they made a difference in this boy's life. To persons suffering from headaches, Sanford posed a spiritual challenge: to affirm that "God's light shines within me and God doesn't have headaches...Every time that we meditate on God's life and light instead of meditating on a headache, we are building into our inner consciousness a new thought-habit of health. Some day that new thought-habit will be stronger than the old one; and headaches will be no more."[9]

Similar visualizations have been used for inner healing and the healing of memories by the evangelical Protestant Ruth Carter Stapleton, sister of former President Jimmy Carter, and Roman Catholic priests Dennis and Matthew Linn. The healing of the spirit involves going back into the place of pain, experiencing the hurt and its impact on your life, and then inviting Jesus to be present in the painful situation. In consciously committing the negative past to God, its power to control is broken.[10]

Affirmative visualizations can make the difference between success and failure in the classroom and in parenting. Studies have indicated that regardless of intelligence and talent, those students who are perceived as low achievers by their teachers perform at a lower level than those who are perceived to be good students. Conversely, those students whose teachers view them as successful learners typically meet their teachers' greater expectations. Inviting a child to visualize her- or himself as successful at sports or learning empowers that child first to see her- or himself as competent and successful and then to achieve that same level of excellence. As a little league baseball and youth basketball coach for many years, I used imagery to enhance my players' senses of confidence and competence as I invited them to see the bat and ball connecting with each other and the basketball going into the hoop with "nothing but net." I also invited them to see themselves as successes, regardless of the outcome of the game.

In my own classroom teaching, in addition to my intercessory prayers on behalf of my students prior to each class, I visualize myself and the students as surrounded by the light of God as I pray for divine guidance on the way to the classroom. I imagine myself speaking clear and insightful words to them. Such visualizations enable me to teach for success rather than failure and to enable students to discover their own unique gifts. To elaborate on an earlier comment, in the moments before I enter the sanctuary to preach and celebrate communion, I visualize God speaking the living word through me and imagine the congregation awakening to God's love and challenge in a new way. If I am speaking to an unfamiliar crowd, I typically identify one or two persons as partners and cocreators in my talk. In the silence as I await my host's introduction, I pray that my words will change their lives for the best and that we will be spiritually joined as conscious members of the body of Christ. In my own experience, the invocation "Let the words of my mouth and the meditations of my heart by acceptable in thy sight, O Lord, my strength and redeemer" prepares the minds, emotions, and nervous systems of the pastor and congregation to attend to God's presence in the words of scripture and the sermon.

Knowing that words can cure or kill, political activist/minister Jesse Jackson leads young inner-city children in the chant, "I am somebody." In inner-city neighborhoods where young children hear the sounds of gunshots and plan for their funerals long before they have reached adolescence, Jackson's words invite them to visualize themselves as children of God, filled with infinite possibilities. Empowered by their affirmation "I am somebody," these children are given an alternative vision of themselves and the surrounding urban reality. Even though poverty and hopelessness may surround them physically, they now see themselves as potential physicians, ministers, accountants, and civic leaders. As they are renewed by the transformation of their minds, they are no longer tempted to conform to the death-filled behaviors of their communities. The violence characteristic of inner-city life no longer becomes their ultimate reality. Their beliefs empower their actions and lead their steps from the inner city to the Ivy League. The affirmation of a positive image, "I am somebody," is an antidote to fear, peer pressure, and low self-esteem and is more potent in the process of transformation than merely a negative statement such as "Just say no."

Still others combine dance and movement with prayerful affirmations. Affirming that the word became flesh, they move with the spirit of the affirmations of faith. Each Sunday, many Christians sing their faith. The words of favorite hymns and psalms become their companions in their dark nights of the soul or in the anguish of illness. Each day as I begin my morning walk, I sing the praise hymn: "This is the day/this is the day/that the Lord has made/that the Lord has made...this is the day that the Lord has made/I will rejoice and be glad in it/this is the day/this is the day/ that the Lord has made." I have found that beginning the day with gratitude enables me to see opportunities even in difficult situations.

Affirmations of faith and creative visualizations were at the heart of Jesus' ministry. "You are the light of the world," Jesus proclaimed to his followers. To vacillating Peter, Jesus affirmed a new name: "You are the Rock on which I will build my church." Perhaps, in his own times of trial, Peter found courage as he remembered and repeated what Jesus had told him years before, "I am a rock...I am a rock...I am a rock...rock solid in my faith."

Jesus invited lepers and sinners to see themselves as God's children. Jesus empowered women to see themselves as disciples and companions in the faith, and, with that new perspective, women received the first great commission and led many of the early Christian house churches. Jesus became the object of faith that cured a woman of a twelve-year chronic illness. As she plunged through the crowd, she repeated over and over, "If I just touch his garment, I will be healed." In reponse to her faith, healing energy flowed forth from Jesus. "Your faith has made you whole," Jesus proclaimed to her.

Jesus' affirmative and inclusive love changed the bodies and the souls of all those he healed, but he also changed their places in the social order. I believe that Jesus brought wholeness to many persons simply by enabling them to see themselves as he saw them—children of divine light, infinitely loved, loving and lovable, creative, and able to begin again and again and again. No longer dominated by images of illness and social ostracism, they found new lives as God's beloved children. This is how Jesus sees you as well!

Faith lives by its affirmations and dies by its negations. Sadly, the message of Christ that welcomed women as spiritual leaders was conformed to the world of sexism and patriarchy. Phobic divisiveness has displaced spiritual hospitality. Tragically, the inclusive message of love and healing was dominated by a guilt-and-blame theology that saw illness as divine judgment and doubt as the doorway to damnation. Faith becomes diabolical when it lives off dead doctrines and forgets its wellsprings in living affirmations of faith. When the church lives by abstract and lifeless doctrines, it succumbs to the worldly separation of saved and damned, insider and outcast, friend and foe. In our worries about our own sin and salvation, we often project evil and immorality onto others. In contrast, the affirmative gospel of Jesus knows no boundaries—lost sheep are found, prodigal children are welcomed home, and broken lives are healed by the vision of our dynamic God, who is "the circle whose center is everywhere and whose circumference is nowhere." This is truly good news! Secure that God loves us, we extend that same love to the persons around us.

It is my belief that the use of faithful affirmations is the basis of the dynamic, relational, and holistic spirituality we need today. As Christians, we need more than once-a-week sermons and Bible studies to nurture our faith and service in a chaotic and challenging world. We need an easily learned, relevant, and accessible form of spiritual practice that gives life to every aspect of faith. We need a spiritual practice that unites tradition and innovation, theology and practice, silence and action. To be holistic, spiritual formation must address and transform the whole of a person's life—parenting, vocation, family, marriage, health, embodiment, and service. I believe that the daily use of affirmations of faith can renew our minds and transform our lives.

The use of affirmations is as old as the biblical tradition itself. The apostle Paul urges his followers to "pray without ceasing." The psalmist invites his companions to meditate on the law of God, working in all things, throughout the day. In recent years, the daily use of affirmations has been at the heart of religious movements as diverse as Faith at Work, Guideposts, the Unity School of Christianity, Upper Room, the positive thinking of Norman Vincent Peale, and the possibility thinking of Robert Schuller. At the ascending edges of the twenty-first century, the use of creative and faithful affirmations provides a theologically sound spiritual discipline for our time.

To elaborate on my earlier comments, living by your affirmations involves the repetition of certain statements whose purpose is to "make firm" your perception of reality. In the heartfelt repetition of affirmations of faith, we experience the Christian vision of reality not only in our minds but also in our hearts, not only in the conscious mind but also in the unconscious mind. We discover that faith is both a process and a relationship, embracing personal growth and intimacy with God and our neighbor. Our faith may even make us whole—physically as well as spiritually. Christian affirmations of faith present an alternative reality to the often negative, materialistic, and individualistic affirmations of the world. At first glance, such affirmations—for example, "God is healing my life," "I am a beloved child of God," "I am strong in the Lord"—may seem unrealistic and counterfactual, especially when our predominant daily experiences are fear, illness, or low self-esteem. Although the use of affirmations does not deny the "shadow side" of life or the rampant injustice of our world, affirmations of faith point us toward a deeper reality within which even the negative aspects of life can be embraced. Affirmations invite us to experience our deepest personal realities as dynamic, imaginative, and empowered children of the living God. As we go beyond the "bad news," we experience the "good news" of a God who is constantly working for good in all things, including our own lives. If we believe that God is at work in our world and that God loves us, then the use of affirmations grounds us in the experience of divine possibility and opens our eyes to God's presence in the most unexpected places.

As we use affirmations, our perception of the world comes to resemble the most deeply held insights of the Christian tradition. We come to see the world through the lens of faith. The reality of all-pervasive divine abundance replaces the illusion of individual scarcity. Events that would intimidate us or alienate us now are seen as opportunities for faithful reconciliation and lively transformation, for now we see challenging events alongside our inspiring affirmations of faith. As we change our minds, we change our hearts, health, actions, and realities. When we use our affirmations, even the fearfulness of death, the separation of ourselves from those we love, loses its sting. Pain, death, and injustice are not denied but placed in the expansive context of God's lively presence within our lives. While we may still "fear" death, we are no longer "afraid" of our "fear"—pain and mortality will not ultimately overwhelm us—as the affirmative words of Psalm 139 become our living theological and emotional reality:

> Where can I go from your spirit?
>   Or where can I flee from your presence?
> If I ascend to heaven, you are there;
>   if I make my bed in Sheol, you are there.
> If I take the wings of the morning
>   and settle at the farthest limits of the sea,
> even there your hand shall lead me,
>   and your right hand shall hold me fast.
> If I say, "Surely the darkness shall cover me,
>   and the light around me become night,"
> even the darkness is not dark to you;
>   the night is as bright as the day,
>   for darkness is as light to you. (Ps. 139:7–12)

In the chapters ahead, I would like to invite you to participate in a lively and tranformative spiritual adventure. I would like to challenge you to take the affirmations of our faith as Christians seriously, to internalize these affirmations, and to let them become the foundation of your perception and action in the world. For many of us, I realize that such a process is a leap of faith. Our doubts are often as great as our faith, but even our doubts can be embraced and renewed as we live by our affirmation that God is as present in the darkness and gloom as in the radiant light. As I struggle toward a new vision of my own vocation, I occasionally doubt that anything good will come of my job transition. I worry about the future and my ability to live out my vocational calling, not to mention paying my mortgage and my son's college expenses! But along with you, I want to commit myself to experiencing the world *as if* the affirmations of our faith are the deepest and most enduring realities of life. By the grace of God, this is what I want and need them to be. I need and want a renewed and transformed mind in which my thoughts and beliefs are in alignment with God's aim for my life. When I do live by these affirmations, my whole world is transformed, and unexpected possibilities emerge. I begin to see the world in terms of God's possibilities and not my own limitations. Even when the external realities have not yet changed, we can experience the movement of God in our lives, growing quietly like the mustard seed in the darkness.

Using affirmations is a call to adventurous companionship with God rather than a return to a narrow doctrinal orthodoxy. The approach of this book is grounded in the spirit of the process-relational theology and philosophy of persons such as Alfred North Whitehead, Charles Hartshorne, and John Cobb. Accordingly, process-relational spiritual formation affirms that spiritual growth is dynamic, contextual, practical, and holistic in nature. Spiritual formation embraces the body and our relationships as well as the spirit. It embraces the earth as well as the heavens. Indeed, the process of spiritual formation involves the ongoing experience of God's lively presence in every aspect of our lives. A process-relational spirituality challenges us to embark on an adventure in which the God beyond and within all our affirmations of faith—the ever-changing and ever-faithful living God who spoke to Moses in the burning bush, who challenged Abraham and Sarah with a new land and new faith, who broke down the wall of separation between Jew and Greek, male and female—leads us to a constantly growing and innovative faith. In aligning ourselves with God's alternate reality, we go beyond narrow and authoritarian dogma to a living faith and partnership of cocreativity with the source of all adventure and evolution. Our use of affirmations is entirely positive: They reflect our faith and joy as Christians rather than our doubts about our own personal abilities or the orthodoxy of our neighbors.

The use of affirmations of faith makes the Bible come alive and liberates scripture from the clutches of stale orthodoxy and irrelevant liberalism. Seen solely in terms of propositional statements and abstract doctrines, the Bible becomes an instrument in the culture wars fought, on one side, by biblical literalists and championed, on the other side, by the Jesus Seminar and historical-critical scholars. In contrast, when the Bible is seen as a vitally alive book of positive affirmations of faith, persons are able to live out the great stories of faith—to begin again with Adam and Eve, to become companions of Abraham and Sarah on the path to a new land, to be liberated from Egypt with the Hebrews, and to experience the healing touch of Jesus along with Jairus' daughter, the woman with a flow of blood, and the man at the pool. In living by biblical affirmations, we embrace the insights of traditional forms of spiritual discipline such as the Rule of St. Benedict and visions of the Spiritual Exercises of Ignatius of Loyola for our time. Turning the pages of scripture invites us to share in Benedictine *lectio divina,* holy reading and meditation, and Ignatian *imaginative visualization,* in which we become characters in the ongoing adventure of biblical spirituality.

In the adventure ahead, we will live by our affirmations of faith. I will invite you to taste, see, speak, sing, dance, walk, and imagine the Christian insights about the providence and omniscience of God, the incarnate presence of God in Christ as transformative of the everyday, the iconoclastic and ever-living Spirit, the holiness of human life and our worthiness of God's light in the world, the empowerment of God in our lives, divine healing, social transformation, the grace of inter-relatedness and community, and the eternal care of God. In living by our affirmations, we will renew our lives. Just as the body is constantly renewed and is—from the cellular point of view—an entirely new creation every few years, the mind is also being constantly renewed as we embrace a healing and transforming vision of reality. In changing our minds, in conforming them to Christ's living presence, we will transform our lives and the world.

The affirmations in this book can be used on either a daily or weekly basis, repeated throughout the year, or merely read through in the spirit of devotional literature. In their holistic interplay of heart, mind, and action, each affirmation will be illuminated by a fourfold pattern:

(1)   an interpretation of its meaning in Christian life in the context of a dynamic, relational, processive perspective, which joins scripture and song;

(2)   a repetition of the affirmation of the day or week;

(3)   a visualization or guided prayer that illuminates the affirmation and breathes life into the repeated word;

(4)   the embodiment of the affirmation in specific commitments to personal growth and social outreach.

In each affirmation, I have also included at least one hymn as part of the process of living your affirmations. I believe that music is one of the deepest forms of holistic theology and spiritual formation as it joins breath, thought, feeling, and motion. Indeed, many of us sing rather than read or recite our deepest affirmations of faith. Although the hymns I have utilized are taken from *Chalice Hymnal,* the majority of them can also be found in the various denominational and ecumenical hymnals. Because the transformation of mind, heart, body, and emotions is essential to living your affirmations, all of your senses can be employed in the affirmations of faith.

My suggestions of affirmations, visualizations, and actions are meant to be a springboard for your own creativity. I ask you to find your own voice and wisdom as you live by these affirmations. In the spirit of some children's books, you can choose your own adventure! I challenge you to embody them in the uniqueness of your own life journey and at your own personal pace. Always remember that affirmations of faith are, first and foremost, a manifestation of God's unconditional grace and surprising creativity. If you forget a day or have trouble focusing on the exercises, don't worry or judge your spiritual journey as deficient. You are always in God's hands, and God is gently leading you toward the divine vision of beauty, goodness, and holiness for your life.

"May you live in interesting times" is an ancient Chinese curse. But for persons of faith, this curse can become a blessing. For those who live by their affirmations of faith, life is always an interesting adventure. We are infinitely interesting in our uniqueness and particular constellation of life events. Our world is interesting with its concrete challenges, temptations, and gifts. And the God of surprising love, whose adventures know no beginning or end, is supremely interesting. Let us live by our affirmations; let us live the adventure of faith in our own "interesting times."

CHAPTER TWO

God's Lively Providence

At the heart of Christian faith is the doctrine of God. We are called to affirm that our faith is grounded in a living reality both within and beyond ourselves and not merely on our subjective experience. Belief is far more than just a placebo. Our character and overall wholeness are given shape and direction over the long run when we have confidence that our beliefs are founded on the solid rock of truth and transformation. Although theology always verges on idolatry when it invokes the name of God too concretely, Christian faith affirms that the living God revealed in the history of the Hebrew people and the life, death, and resurrection of Jesus Christ is also the foundation of the universe and the ultimate source of meaning and security in our lives.

As our understanding of the universe grows and changes, so too does our image of God. While all images of God are finite and partial in nature, certain images of God are tragically toxic and destructive. They nurture feelings of pathological guilt, passive dependence, and fatalistic hopelessness. These beliefs about God may even edge certain persons out of the experience of salvation and wholeness if they absolutize one image, for example, the divine fatherhood to the exclusion of feminine images of God, or divine judgment to the exclusion of divine grace. In the language of Dietrich Bonhoeffer, the German theologian, pastor, and martyr to the faith, many modern persons have pushed God out of their everyday realities. The very nature and character of God has become problematic to them. They identify the image of God with the claims of authoritarian religious and governmental institutions or the ongoing conflict between science and religion. To them, God sanctions the oppressive status quo and the inflexible old-time religion. In their minds, trust in God is equivalent to regression into dysfunctional and moralistic childhood. They no longer have room in their lives for this image of a wrathful, exclusivist, easily angered, and jealous God whose fragile ego is constantly in need of humankind's praise and worship. Nor do they have need of a God whose primary business is punishment in this life and the next based on the orthodoxy of a person's belief system. These images of God are only too real for some persons. Just today, I counseled a university student who admitted that he feared going to hell because many years ago he committed certain minor misdeeds his parochial school teachers had identified with eternal punishment.

As today's spiritual pilgrims discover the spiritual insight and moral integrity of non-Christians such as the Dalai Lama, Thich Nhat Hanh, and Mahatma Gandhi, they find little to worship in a God whose truth and salvation is restricted to a small minority of humankind. A God whose primary admonition to struggling humankind is "turn or burn" has little to say to the moral complexities and spiritual pluralism of our time. Just think of how often you have heard a sensitive and morally upright seeker confess that he or she has jettisoned his or her childhood faith and no longer feels comfortable in the church because of the toxic images of God he or she experienced as a child.

Sadly, images of a distant and arbitrary God characterize the theological reflections of even the most pious of Christians. As a pastor, I hear many believers confess that they don't believe their concerns are important enough to share with God in prayer. Others worry that God will punish them or their children for a youthful indiscretion or a recent exhibition of anger or jealousy. If indeed belief becomes biology, then such images stunt the spiritual, moral, and even physical well-being of believers and agnostics alike.

A tragic reality of Christian history is the continuing abuse of our images of God's relationship to the world. Our creeds and doctrines have become weapons of spiritual warfare rather than instruments of peace and reconciliation. Even the Apostles' Creed, which was fundamental in the shaping of traditional Christianity, has been used often as a means of enforcing abstract orthodoxy and condemning heretics rather than articulating a creative Christian vision of the universe. Further, many believers have failed to recognize that the traditional affirmations of faith are accounts of lively and dynamic images of the divine-human relationship that must constantly be transformed in lively dialogue with our changing world.

We have forgotten that the primary purpose of our affirmations of faith is to express and shape the dynamic and evolving Christian experience of God. Our affirmations become theologically toxic when our concrete and inclusive experience of God's grace and deliverance is replaced by abstract and exclusive rules of belief. Instead of providing reassurance that our lives are in God's hands and "If God be for us, who can be against us?" the robust doctrine of divine omnipotence, for example, became the basis of the disheartening doctrine of double predestination, the belief that God has primordially ordained our salvation or damnation for all eternity. This image of all-determining divine providence encouraged, on the one hand, an infantile submission before God's ordaining will and, on the other hand, a sense of manifest destiny that inspired Europeans to see themselves as God's instruments to bring salvation and culture, not to mention servitude, to the native inhabitants of South Africa and the Americas. The great affirmation "If God be for us, who can be against us?" was interpreted by nationalists and religious imperialists as the sanction for draconian programs of colonization, conversion, and genocide on our continent as well as in Africa and South America, rather than a lively confidence in God's providential love that included and affirmed the insights and worth of native persons. An affirmation of faith is truly an instrument of grace only if it embraces humankind in its transcendence of any select religious, ethnic, or economic group. Life-giving images of God reflect the divine love that overcomes and reconciles all our worldly divisions—Jew and Greek, male and female, rich and poor, saved and unsaved.

Like the doctrine of divine providence, the image of divine creation, intended to affirm the sovereignty of God, the goodness of all creation, and humankind's care and stewardship for creation, has degenerated into a political issue for school boards and combatants in the culture wars of the past century. In their zeal to stamp out the immense journey of biological and cosmic evolution, many Orthodox believers have forgotten the deeper meaning of "creationist" William Jennings Bryan's admonition, "It is more important to know about the rock of ages than the age of rocks!" Liberal Christians have also suffered from a lack of theological imagination insofar as they have failed to articulate a dynamic vision of God's loving providence to match the dynamic stories of universal evolution, quantum physics, holograms, and the Big Bang.

If we are to reclaim the image of the living and creative God in an age of space travel, black holes, carbon dating, and quantum physics, ur images of God must include bold new interpretations of our basic scriptural and creedal affirmations. They must flow out of a creative synthesis of tradition, imagination, experience, and reason in a global and cosmic context.

As Christians, we affirm that our vision of God is defined by the life and teachings of Jesus. When Jesus spoke of God as "our Father," he redefined parenthood—both divine and human. The God who is our "father" is also our "mother." The primary issue in Jesus' revelation of God is relationship, not gender. In speaking of divine parenthood, Jesus invited us to live by our most intimate affirmations and experiences of God's nature. The divine parent of Jesus is known by concrete acts and images of love: the deliverance of the children of Israel from oppression in Egypt; the breaking down of social and religious barriers and the welcome of the outcast; the forgiveness of sins; the healing of the sick; the challenge of exclusivistic, paternalistic, and legalistic forms of religion; and Jesus' own suffering on our behalf. In Jesus' parables, we can visualize God's providence in terms of the growth of a mustard seed and the unexpected discovery of a pearl of great value. These same parables invite us to imagine a shepherd seeking a lost sheep so that the flock might be whole and a father taking the initiative to welcome a lost child home. In Christ, God took on flesh, that we might have abundant lives as persons and participants in God's new social order. The God of the galaxies is also our most intimate companion and guide. In words that are as real in the world of quantum physics as they were in the storyworld of the fathers and mothers of the Christian faith, "God is the circle whose center is everywhere and whose circumference is nowhere."

As the model and embodiment of God's affirmation of both humankind and the created world, Jesus' own vocational and lived affirmations invite us to become God's partners in personal and social transformation:

> The Spirit of the Lord is upon me,
>> because he has anointed me
>> to bring good news to the poor.
> He has sent me to proclaim release to the captives
>> and recovery of sight to the blind,
>> to let the oppressed go free,
> to proclaim the year of the Lord's favor. (Lk. 4:18–19)

This scripture is being fulfilled today for all those who live by the affirmation of God's inclusive, supportive, and transforming love. As we live by our affirmations of God's providence and love, we will see mustard seeds grow into great plants, five loaves and two fishes serve a multitude, and the least of these revealed as God in disguise.

In this chapter's affirmations, we will experience firsthand the transforming reality of God's creativity, love, and providence as we commit ourselves to live daily by our affirmations. As we experience the intimate love of God with heart, mind, spirit, body, and action, we will "taste and see that the LORD is good" (Ps. 34:8). We will also experience the healing of toxic and oppressive images of divinity and the rebirth of divine healing in our lives. When our lives are grounded on the rock of salvation, even in the most challenging of times our hearts will still be singing, for "nothing can separate us from the love of God."

My life flows on in endless song, above earth's lamentation.
I hear the clear, though far off hymn that hails a new creation.
No storm can shake my inmost calm while to that Rock I'm clinging.
Since love is Lord of heav'n and earth, how can I keep from singing?

Through all the tumult and the strife, I hear that music ringing.
It finds an echo in my soul. How can I keep from singing?
No storm can shake my inmost calm while to that Rock I'm clinging.
Since love is Lord of heav'n and earth, how can I keep from singing?

What though my joys and comforts die? I know my Savior liveth.
What though the darkness gather round? Songs in the night he giveth.
No storm can shake my inmost calm while to that Rock I'm clinging.
Since love is Lord of heav'n and earth, how can I keep from singing?

The peace of Christ makes fresh my heart, a fountain ever springing!
All things are mine since I am his! How can I keep from singing?
No storm can shake my inmost calm, while to that Rock I'm clinging.
Since love is Lord of heav'n and earth, how can I keep from singing?

ROBERT LOWRY, "MY LIFE FLOWS ON"

In the days ahead, take time to "taste and see" God's unconditional loving-kindness. As you live by your affirmations, you will discover that God is alive, creating and supporting you in every encounter. You will discover, day by day and moment by moment, that God is working within your life, inspiring you with images of growth and adventure, calling you and the world forward to undreamed-of possibilities. As you live by your affirmations, you will also humbly claim a new role in your daily tasks and responsibilities—the adventure of graceful partnership and co-creation with the God of freedom, creativity, and reconciliation.

Nothing Can Separate Me from the Love of God

> *In all these things we are more than conquerors through him who loved us. For I am convinced that neither death, nor life, nor angels, nor rulers, nor things present, nor things to come, nor powers, nor height, nor depth, nor anything else in all creation, will be able to separate us from the love of God in Christ Jesus our Lord.*
>
> Romans 8:37–39

What are you afraid of? When I lost my job at Georgetown, I lost more than a job. I lost a sense of trust in my employer and confidence in the future. I lost a religious community that I had nurtured in times of bereavement, depression, uncertainty, and questioning. I also lost a community of colleagues that had nurtured me through the death of a parent and the life-threatening illness of a child. In the first few weeks following the notice of my termination, I felt a growing sense of fear, bordering on panic. I was worried that I would repeat the failures of my father, who lost his job in midlife and never quite recovered. I remembered the food baskets my family received and my parents living from paycheck to paycheck. I remembered my father's depression and his inability to secure a meaningful position for many years. Years later, my father still pondered what would have happened to his life "if only" he had kept his position. Deep down in my heart, I wondered if I would ever regain my place in the professional world. Would I always be underemployed or earning a living by piecing together various part-time teaching and pastoral positions?

In the weeks following the termination of my position, the majestic verses of Romans 8 sustained me and gave me courage to live creatively with my personal ambivalence. They helped me to place my life in a wider perspective. My life could not be measured by my fears or even by my achievements, but by God's providential love alone. I learned firsthand that the meaning of divine providence is simply that *our lives are in God's hands, and God is working within the events of our lives to bring fulfillment and joy to us and those we love.*

As I pondered God's providential love, I remembered other situations in which I had found myself at the edge of my endurance and confidence, only to discover that God was with me to sustain my spirit and guide my steps. For years, as an adult living three thousand miles from my parents, one of my greatest fears was the phone call in the night announcing that one of my parents had died and that I would have to take the lonely plane flight from Washington, D.C., to the San Francisco Bay area. When I am under stress, the last place I want to be is in a confined place. In tight spots, claustrophobia kicks in. I feel trapped and impotent.

One evening, the call finally came. My mother had died unexpectedly of a pulmonary embolism following surgery. Initially, I was in such shock that I found it hard to arrange for a flight to the West Coast. I did not sleep much that night, but, by morning, my composure and courage had partially returned as I told my wife that I would make the cross-country flight alone so that she could stay home and celebrate our son's eighth birthday. Still in a state of shock, I felt all right until my wife, Kate, dropped me off at National Airport. As I watched her car speed away, I suddenly felt what a child experiences on the first day of school. I was frightened and lonely. It was only by an act of sheer "adult" will that I boarded the plane that day. But as the plane took off, I was sustained by one of the verses my mother had taught me as a child. No doubt in her own fear, brought on by struggles with self-esteem and obsessive thinking, this verse also sustained her: "Nothing shall separate me from the love of God." Yes, nothing shall separate me from the love of God! That day I was afraid, but my fears did not control me. I believed that whatever happened and however I might feel, I was in God's hands and God would protect me, as I remembered from one of my mother's favorite hymns:

> When peace, like a river, attendeth my way,
> when sorrows like sea billows roll;
> whatever my lot, thou hast taught me to say,
> It is well, it is well with my soul.
>
> HORATIO G. SPAFFORD, "IT IS WELL WITH MY SOUL"

When our son was a young child, he experienced what physicians described as "night terrors." In the middle of the night, he would become terrified as he was caught in the twilight zone between waking and sleeping and couldn't quite find himself in either. It was so terrifying that he was afraid to sleep by himself or even close his eyes at night. When my wife and I could no longer come up with a solution, we called in a child psychiatrist. His words were a balm to my young son's spirit and have stayed with me through the years. "It's okay to be afraid. But you don't have to be afraid of being afraid." I discovered this same reality as my plane sped toward the West Coast. Regardless of how afraid I was, I was still in God's hands. God's eternal love would never forsake me, no matter how frightened I was. I share my story not for the sake of catharsis or even self-revelation, but because I suspect that despite personal or experiential differences, it is your story as well. To all those who experience uncertainty or fear, God proclaims, "Nothing can separate you from my love."

One of the most dislocating passages in life can occur during a young person's first year of college. First-year students have to contend with new roommates, cramped living quarters, making new friends, the chaos of dorm life, different lifestyles, and few enforceable rules in a few short weeks. One year, as Protestant ministry's student leadership team prepared its outreach materials for the first class, one of the student leaders, Jessica Berry, suggested that our motto be "God goes to Georgetown too!" Although she apologized for such a simple theological formula, her words expressed the essence of divine providence and omnipresence. Wherever we are, God is present. In every circumstance, God is working for abundant life for us and everyone else. This was the great discovery of Abraham and Sarah. The God who beckoned them forward was not confined by the borders of their homeland. God would protect, guide, and challenge them in the future as God had done in the past. When they arrived at the promised land, they built altars to the God who was already waiting to bless them there.

Divine providence is not an impersonal and passive force but an active presence working within the challenges of everyday life. In every moment God is leading us forward with the dream of what we can become as God's children. Within the intricate web of relationships, God is confronting us in synchronous moments and unexpected surprises. Nothing can separate us from the dynamic and adventurous love of God!

As Christians, our faith is always communal as well as individual. Our affirmations of faith embrace our neighbor and the stranger as well as ourselves. Nothing can separate *her* from the love of God! Nothing can separate *him* from the love of God! When our son, Matthew, was a senior in high school, he spent a month on an exchange program in Russia. During the Reagan and Bush administrations, peacemakers on both sides initiated student exchanges as a means of enabling Americans and Russians to see one another as human beings and not political caricatures. Although politicians may have spoken of the Soviet Union as the "evil empire," American students discovered that Russian families had many of the same values as their own parents and that Russian students struggled with the same issues of self-identity, sexuality, drugs, and college choices as they did. One group of Americans visualized the Russians as diabolical Darth Vader clones, while the other group visualized them as flesh-and-blood humans with the same dreams as their own. I suspect that the Berlin Wall toppled in the minds of these American and Russian youths and their parents years before its actual collapse. These affirmations of friendship and visualizations of peace may have transformed the minds of Americans and Russians even as their leaders rattled the sabers of chauvinism and alienation.

No one is separated from God's love. I believe that this insight is at the heart of the apostle Paul's counsel to the warring factions in Galatia. "There is no longer Jew or Greek, there is no longer slave or free, there is no longer male and female; for all of you are one in Christ Jesus" (Gal. 3:28). Our affirmation of God's omnipresence and providence challenges us to go beyond religious and ethnic parochialism. All persons are in God's hands. Wherever there is truth and healing, God is present, for in God's house there are many "mansions."

When we affirm, "Nothing can separate us from the love of God in Christ Jesus our Lord," every place becomes home, for every place and every situation is a wellspring of divine providence. Indeed, as we live with this affirmation, we will rediscover the basic trust in the goodness of the universe that many of us lost as children. We will discover God's sustaining presence as we prepare for surgery, face new responsibilities, and confront the evils of our time.

What are you afraid of? In Christ, we are more than conquerors, for nothing in all creation can separate us from the love of God in Christ Jesus our Lord!

EXERCISE ONE: LIVING BY YOUR AFFIRMATIONS

Throughout the day repeat as often as possible the words "Nothing can separate me from the love of God" or "Nothing can separate me from the love of God in Christ Jesus our Lord."

When you begin to feel anxious or stressed, take a moment to repeat, "Nothing can separate *me* from the love of God" as you inhale. Then, as you exhale, let go of the stress and anxiety. Breathe it into the hands of God.

Often our affirmations take on life when we personalize them. In Romans 8, the apostle Paul gives a list of certain situations that might appear to separate us from God's providential love: death, life, angels, rulers, the present, the future, powers beyond our control, heights, and depths. He concludes with the words "nor [can] anything else in all creation...separate us from the love of God in Christ Jesus our Lord." What fears might separate you from the love of God?

Turn your fear into an affirmation. In my own life, the following approach has made God's presence and this scripture concrete and personal as I repeat affirmations such as these: "*The future* cannot separate me from the love of God." "*Unemployment* cannot separate me from the love of God." "*Financial worries* cannot separate me from the love of God." "*Controversy* cannot separate me from the love of God." "*Unfamiliar situations* cannot separate me from the love of God."

Where do you need to experience God's providential care today? Where do you need to experience God's presence and protection? Take a moment to fill in the following affirmations:

_____ cannot separate me from the love of God.
_____ cannot separate me from the love of God.
_____ cannot separate me from the love of God.
_____ cannot separate me from the love of God.

As a companion to this affirmation of divine providence, you might want to affirm Paul's introductory comment when you are facing a difficult situation: "In all...things we are more than conquerors." You might use an affirmation such as the following:

"In Christ, I am a conqueror of my fear of conflict."
"In Christ, I conquer my fear of failure."
"In Christ, I conquer the temptation to overeat."
"In Christ, I conquer my feelings of low self-esteem."

We are not alone in the struggle. God is with us to deliver and heal us.

EXERCISE TWO: LIVING BY YOUR IMAGINATION

Historically, Christian faith has seen the imagination as a spiritual gift. Jesus spoke in parables, which—like the Zen koans—turn the values of the world upside down and reorient us toward God's values. Ignatius of Loyola, father of the Catholic order the Society of Jesus or the Jesuits, saw the imagination as the key to understanding the scriptures. Ignatius invites us, through creative imagination, to become characters in the biblical drama: We experience the healing of the woman with the hemorrhage, the sin of Adam and Eve, the agony of the cross, the denial of Peter. Today, persons with cancer use visualization exercises—such as imaging the divine light surrounding the cancer cells and flushing them out of the body—in order to enhance their sense of empowerment and immune function. I believe that the great creeds of the church come alive when we experience them as the imaginative framework within which we live, move, and have our being. Today, we will experience this affirmation through a guided meditation on the lost sheep (Lk. 15:3–7).

A Meditation on the Lost Sheep. Take a few moments to be still and know that God is with you. Relax your body and mind into God's presence by taking a few deep breaths and experiencing relaxation in your body from head to foot. In the quiet, imagine that you are out in the country, far from city lights. The night is so dark that you can barely see a foot ahead of you as you walk aimlessly. Suddenly, you discover that you are alone and lost. There is no light to guide your way home. How do you feel, being lost in the darkness? Do you stay where you are or continue walking, hoping to find your way home?

Time passes and your meandering in the darkness brings you no closer to home. You call out and no one hears you. In the distance, you hear the howling of wolves and realize that you are defenseless if they attack. Panic rises in your breast as you realize your precarious situation. You begin to ask yourself why you left the safety of the community, the "flock" of your friends and companions. You wonder if the shepherd, or anyone, is looking for you.

Suddenly, in the distance, you hear familiar footsteps. You hear your name being called by a concerned and caring voice. What words does the shepherd use to call you? How does it feel to hear the shepherd approaching in the distance?

At last, the shepherd finds you and carries you back home. What does it feel like to be safe again? What does it feel like to know that the community is incomplete without your presence and that the shepherd loves you so much that he or she will search for you even in the darkest night?

EXERCISE THREE: FAITH IN ACTION

In the words of the epistle of James, "Faith without works is dead." In this same spirit, Martin Luther proclaimed that we are called to be "little Christs" for one another, channeling the grace we have received outward to address the needs of our neighbors. All prayer and doctrine are ultimately "body prayer" and "living faith." Our beliefs not only change our biology and emotional lives, they also change the ways we relate to one another.

While you may choose your own unique way of becoming a channel of divine providence to others, here are some ways to embody, concretely and immediately, the affirmations by which you are living.

(1) In the spirit of Paul's letter to the Galatians (3:28), reflect on the divisions present in our society or your family. Which persons are "separated" from you? Which persons are often classified as "separated from the love of God in Christ Jesus our Lord"? Take time to notice your own personal "outsiders," and pray that you might experience a transformed mind. Ask God to help you see these outsiders as God's own children. Take time to surround them with the light of God.

Divine transformation can change our ways of looking at persons. When Grace Baptist Church in San Jose opened its doors to the Metropolitan Community Church in the 1970s, my sixty-year-old mother was nervous. Her knowledge of homosexual persons was limited to her literal reading of scripture, the discriminatory norms of American society, and her limited knowledge of AIDS. Yet although she was a senior citizen, she was open to change. Although she never felt entirely comfortable with the Metropolitan Church meeting in her church building, she made it a point to reach out to members of the church when they attended the Grace Baptist worship services and potluck dinners. She also became an admirer of the preaching style of the Metropolitan Church's pastor and always had a good word for the church organist, who was also a member of the Metropolitan Community Church. She put her faith into action, and, despite her feelings of discomfort, she chose to embody Christian hospitality to those who had previously been her outsiders.

(2) At the heart of the image of divine providence is the promise "Nothing can separate us from the love of God in Christ Jesus our Lord." Embodying this affirmation challenges us to make a new affirmation: "Nothing can separate this person from *my love* in Christ Jesus my Lord." Ask for God's guidance in identifying persons who need a sense of *your* abiding love and acceptance. Name them before God as you commit yourself to being a channel of the unconditional love that God has given you. In so doing, *you* may become the answer to someone else's prayer.

God Will Supply My Deepest Needs

And my God will fully satisfy every need of yours
according to [God's] riches in glory in Christ Jesus. To
our God and Father be glory forever and ever. Amen.

PHILIPPIANS 4:19–20

"My God will supply every need of yours!" When we suffer any significant change in our lives and relationships, we often begin to think apocalyptically. We begin to imagine the worst-case scenario for ourselves and the world. We may even forget God's providential care for our lives. But the biblical tradition proclaims that there is an alternative to fearful and apocalyptic thinking.

It has been said that there are two primary ways we look at the world: through the eyes of scarcity and fear or through the eyes of abundance and love. When something goes wrong or an unexpected challenge confronts us, most of us are tempted to live by scarcity consciousness rather than prosperity consciousness. Conformed to the values of a culture that lives by the bottom line, we believe that our neighbor's gain is our loss as we compete for time, money, and talent. Our culture's consumerism wants us to believe that we can never have enough time, money, creativity, or intelligence to satisfy our deepest needs. Only by acquiring enough of the right possessions will we be safe from loneliness, economic collapse, or natural disaster. But the fact is that poverty or scarcity consciousness is a matter of perception as much as reality. Think of the millionaires who are convicted of tax evasion or dishonest business dealings. Possessed by their need to accumulate property and power, in their own minds, they never have enough money or a sufficient market share. Think of the person who complains about not having enough friends yet never makes an effort to reach out to strangers. Think of the hours that many of us spend obsessing on tomorrow's financial situation as if it were a matter of life and death. For many of us, the glass is always half empty, regardless of where we stand financially, relationally, or vocationally. We believe that we are alone and unsupported in an essentially uncaring and hostile universe. From this perspective, the only prudent course of action is to "look out for number one." At such moments, we need a transformed mind.

37

A graphic example of scarcity thinking is found in Exodus 16. Shortly after God delivered the Israelites from oppression in Egypt, the people began to complain about their struggles in the wilderness. "If only we had died by the hand of the LORD in the land of Egypt, when we sat by the fleshpots and ate our fill of bread; for you have brought us out into this wilderness to kill this whole assembly with hunger" (v. 3). How quickly they had forgotten the God of deliverance and mercy. The Israelites had become "practical atheists," intellectually acknowledging God's existence, but living as if God's providence were irrelevant to the most basic issues of their lives. Too many of us live this way today!

Despite their lack of faith, God once more supplied the Israelites' deepest needs. "I am going to rain bread from heaven for you, and each day the people shall go out and gather enough for that day…the LORD gives you meat to eat in the evening and your fill of bread in the morning" (vv. 4, 8a). And so, by the loving providence of God, "In the evening quails came up and covered the camp; and in the morning there was a layer of dew around the camp. When the layer of dew lifted, there on the surface of the wilderness was a fine flaky substance, as fine as frost on the ground" (vv. 13–14).

While I affirm the providence of God manifested in the dramatic moments of our lives, I also believe that God's providence is equally present in the ordinary, secular, everyday moments of life. Could the manna have dotted the landscape all along? Could the migrating quail, worn out from their wilderness journey, have surrounded the people all along? Was God already providing for their needs, even while their scarcity thinking blinded them from the gifts of divine providence?

By contrast, our affirmations of faith inspire a prosperity and abundance consciousness that trusts God to provide for all our deepest needs. Just think of the thousands of middle-income families that give over 10 percent of their income to support the church and social justice issues. Although they live modestly, they find ways to support their children's college educations, while their upper-middle-class neighbors take out loans for tuition and housing. Or consider the paralyzed man who chooses to send birthday cards to everyone in his church, makes telephone calls to shut-ins, and ministers with smiles and greetings to the staff and residents of his nursing home. Despite their apparent scarcity, their trust in God's providence has given them everything they need to be happy, fulfilled, and supportive of others.

One of my favorite gospel stories tells of a young boy whose gift of five loaves and two fishes feeds a multitude. This child, alone in a multitude of several thousand, trusts God's providence enough to give up his lunch. Where the multitude saw scarcity, he saw abundance in his modest gift. Did his gift inspire others to share their lunches? Whether the miracle was manifest in Jesus' transformation of the loaves and fish or the transformation of the crowd from scarcity to prosperity consciousness, this boy's small gift was the catalyst for God's blessing on the crowd. Authentic prosperity consciousness involves far more than the glib promises of the "health and wealth gospel" marketed by certain televangelists; it is an attitude of deep trust in God's abiding care and providential love.

If you want to observe an example of fearful poverty consciousness, take the time to watch the local television news. If we took the news literally, we would be convinced that murder, robbery, sexual assault, airline crashes, and automobile accidents were the norm for human experience. From the tone of the news, nothing is safe: Our food, our cars, our religious leaders, and even the news we watch can be hazardous to our health. What we often fail to remember is that these events make the "news" precisely because they are the exceptions to the overall goodness and positive predictability of reality. Despite the tragedies of poverty and violence, most families are happy. Most persons strive to do the right thing in their businesses and relationships. Most teenagers—despite the haranguing prophets of doom—seek excellence in their studies and goodness in their relationships. Each day the basics of our lives are supplied—the sun shines, the planet revolves on its axis, and the atmosphere screens out meteorites and ultraviolet rays. Without our having to lift a finger, the divinely ordained processes of the universe are revealed in the orderly succession of each new day and night.

What would our days be like if we began each morning affirming or singing, "This is the day that God has made, I will rejoice and be glad in it," or with a recapitulation of the Israelites' desert bounty with the hymn "Great Is Thy Faithfulness":

> Great is thy faithfulness, O God my Father,
> there is no shadow of turning with thee;
> thou changest not, thy compassions, they fail not;
> as thou has been thou forever wilt be.
>
> Summer and winter, and springtime and harvest,
> sun, moon and stars in their courses above,
> join with all nature in manifold witness
> to thy great faithfulness, mercy and love.
>
> Pardon for sin and a peace that endureth,
> thy own dear presence to cheer and to guide;
> strength for today and bright hope for tomorrow,
> blessings all mine, with ten thousand beside!

Great is thy faithfulness! Great is thy faithfulness!
Morning by morning new mercies I see;
all I have needed thy hand hath provided—
Great is thy faithfulness, Lord, unto me!

THOMAS O. CHISHOLM, "GREAT IS THY FAITHFULNESS"

"All I have needed thy hand hath provided." In the order and intelligence of the universe, in the seasons of sowing and reaping, in the gentle functioning of the immune and cardiovascular systems, in the forgiveness of sin and the transformation of suffering into joy, experience the tender mercies graciously revealing the omnipresent care of God!

According to the Christian doctrine of omnipresence, God is not an absentee landlord or a Saturday father; rather, God is guiding, inspiring, and re-creating us gently and subtly in every moment of our lives. While God's providence is not all-determining, God's care is all-inspiring and all-encompassing. God is constantly providing a way where there is no way, an alternative vision of the future when all we see is a dead end, a synchronous encounter that will guide us to a new life. Jesus stands at the door and knocks. The still small voice echoes in sighs too deep for words. Beauty assails us at every turn. But we are all too often too blind to see and too fearful to reach out to the future that God is providing for us.

The Exodus 16 passage also contains an interesting message on stewardship. The children of Israel are told to gather all the quail and manna that they need for enjoyment and sustenance. But if they gather more than their fair share or hoard their bounty, it will spoil. If we are good stewards of God's creation, there will be enough food, water, air, and prosperity to go around. Without being oversimplistic, the razing of the rain forests, the destruction of the ozone layer, the pollution of the environment, and the vast economic inequalities of our time are symptoms of our own poverty consciousness and our inability to trust God to supply our deepest needs. Experts on world hunger have long maintained that massive starvation is primarily the result of human choices and not merely scarcity of resources. Benevolent stewardship of God's resources and appropriate distribution of the earth's bounty will provide enough food for every child on the planet. Yet in our fear and poverty consciousness, we hoard the wealth of the earth and consume its bounty before our neighbors can wrest it from us.

The biblical tradition of stewardship calls us to distinguish between what we *want* and what we *need.* When Jesus invites, "Ask, and it will be given you; search, and you will find; knock, and the door will be opened for you" (Mt. 7:7), he is not promising to fulfill our every desire for money, power, or prestige. Rather, he is challenging us to prayerfully bring our needs and desires before God in anticipation that God's wisdom will reveal the deepest desires of our often-restless hearts.

Jesus' words recorded in the Sermon on the Mount invite us to a deep spiritual examination of conscience, in which acknowledging God's care becomes the basis for discerning the difference between needs and desires. "But if God so clothes the grass of the field, which is alive today and tomorrow is thrown into the oven, will he not much more clothe you—you of little faith?...Indeed your heavenly Father knows that you need all these things. But strive first for the kingdom of God and his righteousness, and all these things will be given to you as well" (Mt. 6:30, 32–33). This is not counsel to settle for less in life. The birds of the air and the lilies of the field declare God's glory and reveal God's aim for beauty. God also wants us to experience beauty.

Jesus was known and criticized for his joyful table fellowship. Jesus did not ask the guests at the wedding feast to drink cheap wine, but provided the best wine in great abundance. God wants us to enjoy, but, as theologian David Griffin asserts, "God wants us *all* to enjoy" the bounties of the earth. This universal commitment requires us to see our needs and desires in the context of the well-being of our human and nonhuman companions in God's creation. If we truly trust God to supply our needs, then we will not substitute materialism for relationship, or hedonism for spiritual ecstasy. We will use our gifts with a pure and loving heart, knowing that the God who has been "our help in ages past" will be our "hope in years to come."

God will supply our needs. God is the source of abundance both in resources and in the consciousness that enables us to share our resources with others. God is constantly creating a world of bounty. The world of entropy and scarcity is constantly being replenished and overcome in the open system of divine providence. God is constantly inspiring us to see the beauty and support that is all around us. The renewed and transformed mind is the one that has broken free of the world's shackles of isolation, scarcity, and competition and discovered God's world of relationship, abundance, and partnership.

In my own life, I am discovering day by day that God is working for prosperity and abundance. Perhaps you have discovered the same thing. As I face my own feelings of isolation and scarcity, I discover the bounty of unexpected inspirations, supportive friends, and exciting possibilities. This is not the magic thinking that assumes that God will provide everything while I wait passively. Nor is it leaning on fate to determine unilaterally the events of my life. It is the confident trust that as I work each day to draw closer to God, to maintain a positive attitude and an active spirituality, and to seize the possibilities that come my way both for myself and others, God will provide everything that I need for myself and others. We are all cocreators and partners with the source of every good gift. In ways that we cannot foretell in this life and the next, God is now supplying our deepest needs. Thanks be to God!

EXERCISE ONE: LIVING BY YOUR AFFIRMATIONS

Take some time each day to repeat the affirmation "My God will supply my needs" as a shield and inspiration. In your own spiritual affirmations, concretize this affirmation by relating it to your daily needs. In my own spiritual formation, I have personalized this affirmation by stating: "My God will supply my need for *new vocational possibilities.*" "My God will supply my need for *creative writing ideas.*" "My God will supply my need to *support my son's college education.*" "My God will supply my need to *grow spiritually in this time of challenge.*"

In what ways would you concretize this affirmation? Take some time to create your own affirmations of faith.

"My God will supply my need for _____."
"My God will supply my need for _____."
"My God will supply my need to _____."
"My God will supply my need to _____."

Then, take time to conclude the apostle Paul's affirmation as you recognize the unexpected and bountiful grace of God at work in your life, whether or not you acknowledge it. "My God will supply my need *according to God's riches and glory in Christ Jesus.*"

EXERCISE TWO: LIVING BY YOUR IMAGINATION

Jesus challenged us to "ask, seek, and knock." This process of prayerful asking not only connects us with God's personal guidance but also enables us to discover the deepest desires of our hearts. This deepest desire of our hearts, I believe, is our personal incarnation of the intimate voice of God that enables us to discern our needs from our wants.

In this twofold process of imaginative prayer, the first step is to reflect in silence on the question, What do I really desire in life? Let the images and words emerge without judgment or criticism. Then, continue the process by writing these desires down in your personal prayer journal. In the days ahead, take time to reflect on this list, opening to divine guidance in order to distinguish between your superficial wants and your deeper spiritual desires. Once again, in the silence, let the words and images of your deepest desires emerge. How does this list differ from your initial list? What deep desires do your needs point toward?

For example, my initial desire for a position paying $100,000 a year may, in fact, reflect a much deeper desire for meaningful work. My desire for personal acclaim may reflect a deeper desire to make a positive and creative difference in the lives of others through excellence in my writing and vocation.

As you discover what your deepest desires are, the second step is to begin to image these deep desires: What do they look like? How are they embodied in the world? Where do they fit in relation to God's aim for your life and the needs of the world around you? As your deepest desires are clarified, visualize or name them one by one. Then, place each desire in the "hands of God," allowing God to experience, evaluate, and bless your deepest desires. Conclude by envisaging God as your constant companion and support (using whatever image of God is lively for you, e.g., parent, light, Jesus) in your embodiment of your deepest desires.

Augustine once stated, "Our hearts are restless until they find their rest in God." Our deepest desires, in similar fashion, find their fulfillment only in relationship with God and our neighbor. God's aim is that we flourish at every level of life—mind, body, spirit, relationships, and material well-being. But God also wants abundant life for all persons. To achieve our deepest desires we must also enable others to experience the deepest desires of their own hearts.

EXERCISE THREE: FAITH IN ACTION

As I stated earlier, the Protestant reformer Martin Luther asserted that the Christian is called to be "a little Christ," a channel of grace who gives to her or his neighbor out of the bounty that she or he has received. In so doing, we discover that *we can be the answer to someone's prayer; we can be the incarnation of divine love and abundance in the life of another.* In this spirit, prayerfully ask God to guide you to those persons to whom you can mediate abundant life.

Following his experience with a serious operation, our college-aged son, Matthew, committed himself to volunteering as a big brother for a child with cancer. There is no one path for our channeling of God's grace. Just as God's grace is unique and intimate, our response to that grace is equally personal. It has been said that we discern God's will when we read the Bible in one hand and the newspaper in the other. While I would add prayer, meditation, and communal reflection to this equation, I believe that God calls us through the concrete needs of our communities as well as through random encounters and intuitive insights.

Your experience of God's abundance may call you to share your prosperity by serving food at the local food bank or soup kitchen, wielding a hammer for Habitat for Humanity, signing petitions for Amnesty International to ban landmines, or calling your political representative on an issue of economic, social, or ecological justice. You may be called to protest against sweatshop labor or violence in the media. In the interplay of intimate prayer and personal service to our neighbors, human and nonhuman, we are called both to "think globally and act locally" and "act locally and think globally." Still, whether your outreach is with a hammer or a pen, it is important that you visualize the face of one who represents the needs of those you are serving. God calls us to concrete acts of love—to see the divine face in all its unlikely disguises—and not merely abstract benevolence. We are called to write the check, but also to touch the person.

One way to integrate visualization and action is to imaginatively surround the ones you are serving with God's transforming light. For example, a young adult sponsoring a child through the Christian Children's Fund could place the child's picture in his room and use that picture as an icon for his or her daily prayers. Or, if you are serving food at the soup kitchen, as you ladle eggs or grits onto the homeless persons' plates, take a moment to bless each one as they walk down the line. See each one as a child of God. In this way, you will come to understand that the abundant love of God that led to the cross and resurrection was not for humankind in general but for real struggling persons like the one who stands before you.

In this creative interplay of affirmation, visualization, and action, we discover that all prayer must eventually become *body prayer* as it is lived out in transformed minds and transformed social and personal structures and relationships. Truly, God is supplying my needs. And by God's bountiful love, we are all divine channels supplying the needs of one another.

God Is Always with Me

Where can I go from your spirit?
  Or where can I flee from your presence?
If I ascend to heaven, you are there;
  if I make my bed in Sheol, you are there.
If I take the wings of the morning
  and settle at the farthest limits of the sea,
even there your hand shall lead me,
  and your right hand shall hold me fast.
If I say, "Surely the darkness shall cover me,
  and the light around me become night,"
even the darkness is not dark to you;
  the night is as bright as the day,
  for darkness is as light to you.

PSALM 139:7–12

Where shall I go from God's spirit? For many years, a member of the university faculty where I teach had suffered from severe depression. He had received the best of psychiatric care but still found it virtually impossible to go to work when the darkness of depression engulfed his spirit. One afternoon, our weekly faculty-staff meditation group, "The Still Point," reflected on the passage from Psalm 139. During our time of sharing he related how Psalm 139 had been a spiritual lifesaver for him in times of deepest depression.

> I know what the psalmist is talking about. I have been in the darkness. I have wanted it to cover me so completely that I could never be found again. But in the deepest darkness, this scripture reminded me that God was with me. I have lived those words, "even the darkness is not dark to you, for night is as bright as the day, for darkness is as light to you," for I found a sustaining companion who helped me trust that the darkness would not defeat me.

The personal meaning of the doctrine of divine omnipresence is simply this: *Wherever I am and whatever my circumstances, God is with me.* The doctrine of omnipresence responds to our deepest need for

45

basic trust in the universe. Despite all that threatens our well-being, we are ultimately safe and secure. As children, we experience this deep need when our nighttime fears are met with a parent's reassuring voice and gentle touch: "You are safe. I won't leave you. Even when I'm in the next room, I can hear you." In the midst of their own fears about the future, the disciples heard that same promise from Jesus: "Lo, I am with you always, even until the end of the age."

The traditional doctrine of divine omnipresence cannot be abstracted from the other traditional descriptions of God—as divine power, creativity, knowledge, and love. God's presence is always an effective, creative, intimate, and saving presence. The words of Psalm 139 pertain to the whole of life: In joyful ascending to the heavens, God is with us; in despairing moments of failure and isolation, God is with us; even when we would seek to cover ourselves with the darkness of self-destruction, God is also with us.

A woman whose daughter committed suicide after struggling for many years with depression came to me with the question, "Where is Judy now?" She feared that her daughter's self-destructive death would negate God's care for her. In response, I reassured her with the affirmation that God is with us in every possible life condition and that God's faithful care remains steadfast even beyond the grave. God was with Judy when she took her life, and God is with Judy in the great adventure of eternity where, I believe, all the woundedness that led to her suicide will be healed. A contemporary hymn portrays the personal meaning of divine omnipresence.

> I was there to hear your borning cry, I'll be there when you are old.
> I rejoiced the day you were baptized, to see your life unfold.
>
> I was there when you were but a child, with a faith to suit you well;
> in a blaze of light you wandered off to find where demons dwell.
>
> When you heard the wonder of the word I was there to cheer you on;
> you were raised to praise the living God, to whom you now belong.
>
> If you find someone to share your time and you join your hearts as one,
> I'll be there to make your verses rhyme from dusk till rising sun.
>
> In the middle ages of your life, not too old, no longer young,
> I'll be there to guide you through the night, complete what I've begun.
>
> When the evening gently closes in and you shut your weary eyes,
> I'll be there as I have always been with just one more surprise.

I was there to hear your borning cry, I'll be there when you are old.
I rejoiced the day you were baptized, to see your life unfold.

JOHN YLVISAKER, "I WAS THERE TO HEAR YOUR BORNING CRY"

One of my favorite gospel stories, the storm at sea (Lk. 8:22–25), illumines God's omnipresent care. As the wind and waves pummel their boat, the disciples cower in fear, for they have forgotten that Jesus is with them. When they finally remember that Jesus is with them, Jesus awakens and then commands the waves, "Peace, be still!" As the storm subsides, Jesus asks his followers, "Where is your faith?" When we remember that God is with us in every challenging moment, we will no longer be afraid of our fears and anxiety, for God's presence will be with us regardless of what occurs.

EXERCISE ONE: LIVING BY YOUR AFFIRMATIONS

Take some time to repeat, verbally or silently, one of the following affirmations: "God is with me." "I am always in God's presence." "Wherever I am, God is there also." "God is with me in the storm and darkness."

To concretize this affirmation, relate it to the events of your current life. In my own case, for example, I have used this affirmation as a source of confidence and strength in a number of settings: "God is with me in *this interview.*" "God is with me as *I confront a difficult coworker.*" "God is with me in *my fears.*" "God is with me as *I grieve a friend's death.*" "God is with me as *I give this lecture.*"

Take time to reflect on those situations where you might need God's presence, only to discover, like the person in the poem "Footprints," that all along God has been carrying you!

"God is with me in _____."
"God is with me in _____."
"God is with me as _____."
"God is with me as _____."

EXERCISE TWO: LIVING BY YOUR IMAGINATION

Today, many persons, to quote the author Walker Percy, feel "lost in the cosmos." Displaced by science and technology from the center of the universe, they feel disconnected, unimportant, and alone. Yet if God is omnipresent, then every place is the center of the universe, for "God is the circle whose center is everywhere and whose circumference is nowhere." When we discover that God is with us, every place becomes home. In the following guided meditations, you are invited to find God's presence in the most unexpected places.

A Meditation on the Darkest Place. In the quiet, think of the darkest place imaginable. What is it like to be in this dark, apparently godforsaken place? What are your fears in the darkness? What dark moments are you facing today? What has brought you to the darkness?

In the midst of the darkness, you discover a flickering light in the distance. Gently and slowly, the light begins to illumine the darkness. This light is the light of God that no darkness can conquer. How do you feel as the light begins to illumine the darkness? What do you see now in what once was pitch darkness? What blessings are present in the illumined darkness?

Close this time of meditation with a moment of thanksgiving for the gift of divine light even in the darkest moments of your life.

A Meditation on the Storm at Sea. Read reflectively the words of Luke 8:22–25. Let the words soak deep into your spirit. What are they saying to you today?

In the quiet, imagine a beautiful, sunny day. You and a number of your best friends are taking a voyage across the Sea of Galilee. You are celebrating your recent successes as a spiritual group. Imagine the scenery. Feel the sunshine and the gentle wind. Who is traveling with you? What provisions have you brought for your celebration on the water? Your mood matches the weather as you gently skim across the waves.

Suddenly, in the midst of your celebration, you notice that the sky is turning black, the wind is beginning to howl, and lightning strikes in the distance. Visualize the impending storm as it becomes stronger and more threatening until your sailboat is engulfed by the raging storm and tumultuous sea. How do you feel as the storm buffets your sailboat as if it were a toy? Experience the chaos and fear that the storm brings.

What storm is going on in your life these days? What are your emotions as you experience this storm? What resources do you have as you face the storms of life?

As the storm rages, you cry out to God, forgetting that Jesus is with you. But then you turn around and remember that Jesus has not abandoned you, but is quietly sleeping in the boat's cabin. How do your emotions change when you discover that Jesus is in the boat with you?

Jesus suddenly emerges from the cabin and simply commands the storm, "Peace, be still." The storm calms, the light returns, and you sail toward home propelled by a gentle wind. All is well. Note your emotions now. Claim your positive emotions and seek to affirm them the next time you are afraid—the next time you experience a storm in your life.

As you come forth from your meditation, take a moment to thank God for God's care and presence in the raging storms of your life.

EXERCISE THREE: FAITH IN ACTION

We are challenged to give what we have received. The God with us in the storms of life is also with others. As I noted earlier, it has been said that there are only two kinds of people in the world: those who are in God's hands and know it, and those who are in God's hands and do not know it. Although God's love is our constant companion, often—like the disciples in the storm—we feel alone and without resources. Our task as Christians is to share the simple gospel message "God is with you always." We are called to be the incarnation of God's presence by our words and deeds for those who struggle and despair amid the storms of life. In our love, we become the basic trust that enables a struggling seeker to experience the universe as friendly and supportive, despite its challenges.

In your own life, there are persons whose lives call you to service and care, persons for whom your presence may make the difference between life and death. Ask God to reveal those who need your care. Name them in your daily prayers. Ask for God's wisdom to respond creatively and supportively to the needs of those who struggle in the darkness. As you give them a sense of divine companionship, your own sense of God's presence will be multiplied.

God Knows Me and Loves Me

O LORD, you have searched me and known me.
You know when I sit down and when I rise up;
*   you discern my thoughts from far away.*
You search out my path and my lying down,
*   and are acquainted with all my ways.*
Even before a word is on my tongue,
*   O LORD, you know it completely.*
You hem me in, behind and before,
*   and lay your hand upon me.*
Such knowledge is too wonderful for me;
*   it is so high that I cannot attain it.*

PSALM 139:1–6

One of humankind's greatest needs is the desire to be known intimately. Today, many persons and corporations have objective information about us. Our credit histories are available in the blink of an eye to banks, credit companies, and mortgage bankers. At the touch of a computer key, law enforcement agencies can access our driving records. Our lives are constantly under the scrutiny of governmental agencies and business concerns. We fear being audited by the IRS. Although they may have minute information about our lives, none of these agencies really know us. Sometimes, their knowledge feels like a violation of our privacy. At other times, the objective and unfeeling data on our credit reports leave us feeling vulnerable and misunderstood. Merciless in their objectivity, they cannot truly understand a missed payment or a credit renegotiation. No numbers on a credit report or a tax return can describe the financial and emotional dislocation caused by a spouse's terminal cancer, a divorce, the loss of a job, or a parent's Alzheimer's disease, nor can a medical chart in its objectivity describe the wholeness of a hospital patient's life.

We all desire the intimacy of being known. But we are often deeply afraid of intimacy. Too often, the knowledge that others have about us is held against us. Too often, we are embarrassed about the most intimate details of our lives. We worry that if our girlfriends, neighbors, or spouses really knew us, they would ridicule or abandon us. In certain counseling

50

settings, I have found that my parishioners often trot out their dirty laundry early in the session. Subconsciously, they may want to shock their pastor, who—of course—they assume is innocent in the ways of the world. But beneath the shock value, they may desire to know their pastor's breaking point. In their own hearts they are asking, How much can I reveal before she gives up on me as being immoral and beyond redemption? Will he turn his back on me if he discovers that I am a homosexual, fantasize about leaving my spouse, or have doubts about the historic creeds of the church? This same pattern occurs when we begin to date someone new: We begin with superficial details and then, as the trust level deepens, choose to reveal more personal aspects of our lives, hoping that when they have heard our worst fears and most intimate secrets, they will still love and accept us.

Many of us fear God's knowledge of our lives. We imagine that God is some sort of Peeping Tom, who peers through the windows of our lives in order to catch us in a morally dubious situation. Or we identify God with the state trooper, hiding behind a billboard, poised to ticket us for speeding. Or we visualize God as the stern, black-robed hanging judge for whom no penalty is too severe. In our fear, we confess, "If God really knew who we were, God would surely damn us!" Such visions of divine omniscience portray God as a vengeful demon whose punishment far outweighs the crime. Such a God never accepts excuses or considers extenuating circumstances. "A rule is a rule; there are no exceptions," this God pronounces to anyone seeking understanding and forgiveness. Distant and austere, this God only knows us objectively. Unsympathetic, this God is hardly concerned with the complexities of moral decision making, the ambivalence of the heart, and the impact of the environment on our lives.

With all our fears of intimacy, most of us still spend our lifetimes in search of someone who will accept us, someone whose love will never fail us. We also yearn for a God to whom we can come "just as I am without one plea," a God whose knowledge of us only adds to "her" care for us.

The words of Psalm 139 celebrate our being known by a very different kind of God. To the psalmist, God's omniscience is defined by God's providential care. Wherever I am, I am known by God. As a toddler explores his expanding world, he constantly pushes beyond his known world; but as he reaches the edges of the known, he gains comfort when he looks back and notices that his father is watching him. Just to be known by one who loves you provides a sense of security. In the toddler's mind, "Dad won't let anything bad happen to me." And when we experience ourselves as objects of the compassionate knowledge of God, we also feel protected and safe. God's loving knowledge accepts us just as we are. We don't need to make excuses; we don't need to hide; and we don't need to pretend to be better than we are. None of these actions will make any difference in terms of God's care for us. Even when the prodigal son journeys to the far country of substance abuse and unsafe sex, his father and mother still love him and look after his best interests "behind the scenes." Although they recognize that he must face the consequences of his misused freedom, we can imagine that these parents are ensuring that there will be a safety net—even if it is a job working for a pig farmer—when their child falls from grace. When he comes to his senses and journeys homeward in shame, his return is not a surprise to his parents, for he has always been the object of their anonymous, but compassionate, gaze. How many loving parents have lived out this parable as they patiently awaited their son or daughter's return home from a far country?

"You search out my path...and are acquainted with all my ways...Such knowledge is too wonderful for me." The psalmist can barely contain the joy he feels at being known by God. In the joyful words of the African American spiritual:

> Why should I feel discouraged, why should the shadows come,
> why should my heart be lonely and long for heaven and home,
> when Jesus is my portion? My constant friend is he:
> his eye is on the sparrow, and I know he watches me...
> I sing because I'm happy, I sing because I'm free,
> for his eye is on the sparrow, and I know he watches me.
>
> CIVILLA D. MARTIN, "HIS EYE IS ON THE SPARROW"

Our trust in God's loving knowledge is the foundation of our personal and corporate prayer lives. We pray because we believe that God is listening and that our lives really matter to God, not as objective data, but as flesh-and-blood experiences. We pray because our prayers make a difference to God. We pray to remind ourselves that we are known. To be known by God enables us to risk knowing ourselves. The power of the psalms is that the psalmist shares everything with God—anger, disappointment, fear, depression, hatred—the shadowy emotions of life— as well as moments of joy and triumph. In trusting divine omniscience, we are empowered to face our shadow sides and claim the many facets of our personalities. Without the feeling of acceptance, there can be no integrity. The subconscious is too frightening, and the superego is too demanding. But when divine knowledge becomes a lived reality—an affirmation of faith by which we live our lives and interpret our world— we need no longer feel shame, guilt, or embarrassment about who we are. God knows us and loves us just as we are, and now we can love ourselves and let go of our projections onto our neighbors.

For many years I struggled with four verses (vv. 19–22) of Psalm 139. In my desire to claim this psalm as an unambiguously edifying vision of the divine-human relationship, these harsh words seemed anachronistic betrayals of the psalmist's true meaning. I regularly omitted them from public worship and Bible studies. Surely, they must have been a chauvinistic afterthought, included to justify the psalmist's own violence and hatred, I contended.

> O that you would kill the wicked, O God,
>> and that the bloodthirsty would depart from me—
> those who speak of you maliciously,
>> and lift themselves up against you for evil!
> Do I not hate those who hate you, O LORD?
>> And do I not loathe those who rise up against you?
> I hate them with perfect hatred;
>> I count them my enemies.

And then, the passage once more reaches the heights of spiritual aspiration:

> Search me, O God, and know my heart;
>> test me and know my thoughts.
> See if there is any wicked way in me,
>> and lead me in the way everlasting.

Now I believe that, at closer inspection, the venomous ejaculations are as essential to the psalm as the heavenly discourses. The God who searches and knows us—the God whose love I can never escape—is the only God I can trust with my shadow side, my pettiness, hatred, and fear. Even at my worst, I cannot forfeit God's loving care for me. Living by the spirit of the psalm enables me to face myself and find healing, for if God is able to embrace my anger, God is also able to provide for my deepest needs.

Omniscience is not an abstract doctrine. In the concrete world of guilt and shame, failure and alienation, the doctrine of omniscience reassures us that our lives truly matter to God and that God's knowledge is both protective and redemptive. The One who knew his persecutors more intimately than they knew themselves proclaimed with his dying breath, "Father, forgive them, for they know not what they do." While those of us from liberal churches may chuckle at the schmaltzy themes of those evangelical revival hymns of our youth, the healing, life-transforming omniscience of God finds its deepest expression in a hymn used as the "altar call" in the Billy Graham crusades:

> Just as I am, without one plea, but that thy blood was shed for me,
> and that thou bid'st me come to thee, O Lamb of God, I come, I come!
>
> Just as I am, though tossed about with many a conflict, many a doubt;
> fightings and fears within, without, O Lamb of God, I come, I come!
>
> Just as I am, thou wilt receive, wilt welcome, pardon, cleanse, relieve;
> because thy promise I believe, O Lamb of God, I come, I come!
>
> Just as I am, thy love unknown, hast broken ev'ry barrier down;
> now, to be thine, yea, thine alone, O Lamb of God, I come, I come!
>
> CHARLOTTE ELLIOTT, "JUST AS I AM, WITHOUT ONE PLEA"

As we journey from the evangelical to the metaphysical, twentieth-century Anglo-American philosopher Alfred North Whitehead describes the transformative nature of divine omniscience in a similar spirit. Whitehead asserts that God's creativity—that is, God's ability to transform our lives and the world—is intimately related to God's receptivity, God's willingness to share in our imperfections and failures. In contrast to the hanging judge of popular theology, Whitehead sees divine judgment in terms of God's deep empathy and understanding:

> God saves the world as it passes into the immediacy of *God's* own life. It is the judgment of a tenderness which loses nothing that can be saved. It is also the judgment of a wisdom which uses what in the temporal world is mere wreckage...God does not create the world, *God* saves it: or more accurately, *God* is the poet of the world, with tender patience leading it by *God's* vision of truth, beauty, and goodness.[1] (italicized editing for inclusive language)

Our lives truly matter to God. Our lives are written on the palm of God's hand. As a result of the impact of our lives, God's own nature is transformed. Omniscience means that our lives contribute to God's own quality of experience and creative activity. God has a stake in our spiritual growth: Our lives in their entirety are our gift to God. Whitehead holds that our commitment to God enables God to be a different God than God might have been without our prayerful devotion:

> What is done in the world is transformed into a reality in heaven, and the reality in heaven passes back into the world. By reason of this reciprocal relation, the love in the world passes into the love in heaven, and floods back again into the world. In this sense, God is the great companion—the fellow sufferer who understands.[2]

Guided by a truly intimate and personal love, God is the divine circle who "centers" on each of us as if we are the only one and who inspires our own personal "centering" on God. In this divine mirroring, we find the courage to know and love ourselves and let go of our negative projections onto others.

EXERCISE ONE: LIVING BY YOUR AFFIRMATIONS

In order to experience the personal meaning of the doctrine of omniscience, repeat the following affirmation: "God knows me completely and loves me completely."

Personalize this affirmation by concretizing it in everyday life. For example, in my situation I might affirm: "God knows my *anger at the university administration* and loves me completely." "God knows my *fear of failure* and loves me completely." "God knows my *ambivalence about the future* and loves me completely." "God knows *the impact of childhood fears on the present* and loves me completely."

As you concretize the experience of divine loving omniscience, repeat your own variations of this affirmation:

God knows my _____ and loves me completely.
God knows my _____ and loves me completely.
God knows my _____ and loves me completely.
God knows my _____ and loves me completely.

EXERCISE TWO: LIVING BY YOUR IMAGINATION

In recent years, the "healing of memories," pioneered by Roman Catholic priests Dennis and Matthew Linn as well as by Jimmy Carter's sister Ruth Carter Stapleton, has enabled many persons to experience the healing of pain and humiliation of the past. In the healing of memories, we return to the scene of our deep hurt and invite Jesus to experience the pain with us. We let go of the pain as we place it in the hands of our

Savior. This process can be used not only to heal memories but also to confront our anxieties and fears.

It has been said that we are only as sick as our secrets. Often, we hide our deepest secrets even from ourselves. But when we remember the wisdom of the African American spiritual "Nobody knows the troubles I've seen, nobody knows but Jesus," our secrets lose their power over us as we reveal them to the One "to whom all hearts are open and all desires known." The two visualization exercises that follow embody the healing power of divine omniscience.

Healing of a Memory. Take a few moments to be still. You may do this visualization sitting in a comfortable chair or lying down. Perhaps you may use a relaxation exercise to calm your body from head to toe and release the tensions of the day. In the stillness, ask for God's guidance in revealing to you a memory whose pain still shapes your life. Gently and patiently let the words and images emerge in your mind's eye. You may even be surprised by the memory that surfaces.

Visualize yourself in that place of pain. What went wrong? Who were your antagonists? How were you hurt? How did you respond? Do you feel any regret or guilt about your own response? In whatever way is appropriate, experience the feeling tones of that situation.

Now visualize Jesus as your partner in that scene. The One who is with you always and whose love embraces good and evil alike is your healing companion. Share your pain, guilt, anger, or other dark impulses with Jesus. Offer up all your pain and struggle to Jesus. See Jesus' healing light bathe the whole situation, embracing both friend and foe, as it embraces your own life. See Jesus loving those who are hurting you—see their own pain and hurt—even as Jesus is loving you. If you are able, ask Jesus to give you the strength and love to forgive your antagonists and yourself, if necessary. If you cannot marshal the personal resources of forgiveness, simply ask Jesus to bear the pain for you and extend forgiveness on your behalf.

As you conclude this meditation, thank God for the deep love that has been given to you. See yourself journeying homeward with Jesus as your loving companion.

Remember as you practice the healing of memories that there are situations of deep pain that require both human and divine partnership for their healing. Persons who have experienced various forms of spousal, sexual, physical, or ritual abuse may need caring guidance, pastoral, psychiatric, and spiritual, from a variety of sources and possibly medication. Healing of memories can be a lifelong process, requiring the healing of emotions, relationships, and the spirit simultaneously or one sphere at a time. God is at work in every healing modality, including chemical therapy and psychotherapy.

A Meditation on a Secret Pain or Fear. Once again, find a quiet comfortable place. Be still and know that God is with you. In the quiet place, open your heart to your deepest experience. Is there a fear or secret that has kept you in bondage? Might there be a fear or secret that is so painful or embarrassing that you don't even want to admit it to yourself, let alone other persons? Remember that "God has searched and known you" and that God's knowledge of you is grounded in God's love and creativity.

Take a moment to visualize that secret or fear. Experience the feelings associated with it. Visualize Jesus as your companion as you face this fear or secret. Jesus will not judge or abandon you. Let Jesus experience it from inside. Let Jesus experience your own feelings about this fear or secret. How does it feel to have Jesus as your companion? Place your feelings, fears, and secrets in Jesus' hands. Let Jesus bathe them in healing light. Let Jesus love the fears as Jesus loves you. Ask Jesus to give you a healing and a gift from your fears and secrets. You no longer have to be bound by them, because now they are in Jesus' hands.

Conclude this time of visualization with a time of thanksgiving for God's loving awareness of your life.

EXERCISE THREE: FAITH IN ACTION

When someone truly listens to us, we experience healing and affirmation. Perhaps our society's fixation on noise today—our constant need to have the TV, radio, or CD player on—reflects our fear that no one is truly listening to us. We often fill the void of true encounter with chatter and background noise. In contrast, when we take time to "be still, and know that I am God" (Ps. 46:10), we hear not only our own deepest voices but also the deepest voices of our neighbors. When we trust God enough to simply let the other speak, without feeling defensive or needing to fill the empty spaces with words, we hear the other into healing and transformation.

While putting your faith into action, take time to listen—not just with your ears but also with your heart. If you are thrown into conversation with a stranger, family member, spouse, or friend, simply listen. Let their words speak to your heart without judgment or defensiveness. Listen for the inner words of pain, joy, or uncertainty beneath their spoken words. Focus on their words as your mantra—the prayer word that invites you to experience God. Listen for the voice of God speaking through their joys and sorrows. Remember that by your listening and care, you are giving and receiving the love of Christ.

God's Angels Protect and Guide Me

*You who live in the shelter of the Most High,
  who abide in the shadow of the Almighty,
will say to the LORD, "My refuge and my fortress;
  my God, in whom I trust."
For he will deliver you from the snare of the fowler
  and from the deadly pestilence;
he will cover you with his pinions,
  and under his wings you will find refuge;
  his faithfulness is a shield and buckler.
You will not fear the terror of the night,
  or the arrow that flies by day,
or the pestilence that stalks in the darkness,
  or the destruction that wastes at noonday…
For God will command his angels concerning you
  to guard you in all your ways.
On their hands they will bear you up,
  so that you will not dash your foot against a stone.*

PSALM 91:1–6, 11–12

Recently, a friend gave my family a ceramic plaque that read "Angels are watching over our home…guiding our family while together or alone." As twenty-first-century persons awaken to spirituality, angels have become popular. Courses are offered on themes such as how to contact your angels and spirit guides, and angel healing. Unfortunately, many of the courses as well as the popular literature imply that angelic beings exist only to serve humankind and will be at our beck and call regardless of our needs, if we only learn the right communication technique. While the biblical tradition affirms that angels reflect God's providential care for humankind, we must not forget that the scriptures also portray angels as divine messengers whose vocation is to communicate God's guidance and will to humankind. In contrast to the cuddly, benign figures of popular angelology, angels in their role as God's messengers are often frightening and always "awesome." When the shepherds in the field near Bethlehem encounter the angel of the Lord, they quake in fear. The angel reassures them—as the biblical angels often do—with the words "Do not be afraid, for I am bringing you good news of great joy for all people." Isaiah, Mary, and Joseph received reassurance as well as a mission when God's angels visited them.

In the biblical tradition, angels reveal God's truth to humankind and provide God's care for persons in great need. The accounts of angelic visitations remind us that God is constantly providing for our deepest needs. Although God is always with us, the angelic visitors represent a significant aspect of God's omnipresence—the divine desire to constantly communicate God's truth and protection to us in ways that we can experience and understand. There is no need for us to go to workshops, the goal of which is to give us a "spiritual" technique for contacting our own personal angels. We don't need a technique to conjure up the angelic presence. Angels are already among us, but we are often blind and deaf to their voices. In awakening to God's own care, we also awaken to those synchronous and life-changing encounters with the "spiritual world" and its manifestation through dreams, visions, symbols, sacraments, stories, and songs.

As many of today's accounts of angelic visitation point out, God comes to our aid precisely when we are in the greatest need. In Psalm 91, the angels are one manifestation of the circle of love that always surrounds and undergirds us. We always live in "the shelter of the Most High." Whether we know it or not, God is always our "refuge and fortress." Like many of the psalms, the context of Psalm 91 is a time of challenge and conflict. The psalmist is, no doubt, experiencing what today's physicians call the "fight-or-flight response." Terror is all around him— whether it be military conflict, political intrigue, or the threat of another nation. His senses are heightened; his andrenaline is rushing; and he is prepared to defend himself against a malevolent foe. The psalmist is on the verge of panic.

While we seldom face life-threatening situations or hand-to-hand combat in our daily lives, we know the fight-or-flight response as it is elicited by a competitive coworker, an antagonistic parishioner, or an aggressive supervisor. In such moments, we need the guidance and protection that the angelic forces of life provide. We need the refuge and fortress that only God can provide. In the midst of his own internal struggles and external conflicts, the reformer Martin Luther penned the lines of the Protestant Reformation's most definitive hymn, which reflects this caring reality:

> A mighty fortress is our God, a bulwark never failing,
> our present hope amid the flood of mortal ills prevailing.
> For still our ancient foe doth seek to work us woe,

with craft and power great, and armed with cruel hate,
on earth without an equal...
And though this world with devils filled, should threaten to undo us,
we will not fear for God has willed the truth to triumph through us.
The powers of darkness grim, we tremble not for them;
their rage we can endure, for lo, their doom is sure:
One little word shall fell them.

MARTIN LUTHER, "A MIGHTY FORTRESS IS OUR GOD"

Our world may not be populated by literal demons, but we know the feeling of conflict that reflects the diabolical, alienating, and threatening powers of life. With Luther and the psalmist, we know that our own efforts cannot prevail against the internal fear and the external foe. We need, as the twelve-step programs proclaim, a "higher power" who is on our side and ever ready to fight alongside us against the inner addiction and the external temptation. Although some may not appreciate the military language of Psalm 91 or Luther's hymn, real life often involves facing a foe of greater strength or challenging the inner voices of despair. When we seek justice, peace, or personal transformation, we often face both the inner spiritual forces of inertia and the external powers of negativity. At such moments, we need to experience God as being "on our side," within us and around us (Mt. 5:43–48). Yet we must remember not to demonize either the internal or external foe. God's sun shines on the righteous and unrighteous alike.

In the recent film *The Sixth Sense,* a young boy is frightened by his encounters with ghosts. His therapist suggests that rather than running away from the ghosts, he should listen to them. This same approach is at the heart of the nonviolent quest for freedom, articulated in our time by Mohandas Gandhi and Martin Luther King, Jr., which affirms that peace and justice will be achieved only by converting the oppressor through love. With the angels at our side, we can appeal to the "higher angels" of those who threaten us. As we choose love rather than fear, our own spiritual transformation awakens the voices of transformation in others. Although this is often a painstaking process requiring all the patience that we can muster, this process of peacemaking, grounded in the awareness of God's protection, defuses the chaos within and the violence without. God's angels will "guard you in all your ways." This does not mean that we are immune to pain and misfortune. Martin Luther King, Jr., and Mohandas Gandhi both died at the hands of assassins. But it does mean that our lives are ultimately in God's angelic and providential care, and God will have the final word in our lives, and that word is grace. In the words of a popular hymn, inspired by Psalm 91,

And I will raise you up on eagle's wings,
bear you on the breath of dawn,
make you to shine like the sun,
and hold you in the palm of my hand.

MICHAEL JONCAS, "ON EAGLE'S WINGS"

God's providential omnipresence is grounded in the affirmation that God is always with us, providing guidance, insight, protection, and care through a variety of manifestations, human, nonhuman, and divine. God's angels are watching over us, guiding and protecting us wherever we go.

EXERCISE ONE: LIVING BY YOUR AFFIRMATIONS

In your affirmation of divine guidance and providential care, simply live with the promise "God's angels constantly guide and protect me." In my own affirmations, I have concretized this with phrases such as: "God's angels guide and protect me as *I attend this meeting.*" "God's angels guide and protect me in *this interview.*" "God's angels guide and protect me as *I plan for the future.*"

Take a moment to reflect on how you might concretize the affirmation "God's angels guide and protect me."

God's angels guide and protect me in _____.
God's angels guide and protect me in _____.
God's angels guide and protect me as _____.
God's angels guide and protect me as _____.

EXERCISE TWO: LIVING BY YOUR IMAGINATION

Take a few moments to relax and be still. Let go of the cares of the day. Ask for God's guidance in the moments ahead.

Reflect on a situation in your life in which you feel conflict, defensiveness, fear, or perplexity. Visualize the situation. Visualize the source of your conflict and anxiety. Take a few moments to experience your feelings in this situation.

In the midst of the conflict, you feel a holy presence, a divine angel. Image this angel—this messenger of God—in a way that seems comfortable or appropriate. This angel is not alone, but is accompanied by a "multitude of angels." One by one, the angels gather in a circle around you. No internal or external foe can penetrate this angelic forcefield. How does it feel to be surrounded by the angels? How does the conflict seem from this perspective?

As they surround you in protection and care, the angels bestow on you a word of guidance, a word from God speaking directly to this situation of conflict. What word of guidance do you receive? How does it feel to know that God's guidance is always with you?

Once again, relax in the silence. Conclude with the prayer that you will be aware of God's protection and guidance in future conflict situations and that you will remember the guidance that you have received today. Close with a prayer of gratitude for God's providential care.

EXERCISE THREE: FAITH IN ACTION

You can be the answer to someone's prayer. You can be someone's "angel," that is, a manifestation of divine care, protection, and guidance. Take some time to reflect on a person who needs your care. Commit yourself to showing that care in a humble and nonintrusive manner, guided only by God's wisdom.

Take some time also to reflect on defenseless persons in our society (children, unwed mothers, homeless, mentally ill, impoverished elders). Ask God to direct you to care for the defenseless by your social and political involvement. In your political life, reflect on governmental policy as it relates to the "least of these." Contact your representatives at local, state, and national levels with your concerns for issues that involve the defenseless and powerless in our cities, nations, and world. You can be an "angel," a messenger of glad tidings of great joy to someone in need.

God's Goodness Creates My Life

> *In the beginning when God created the heavens and the
> earth, the earth was a formless void and darkness covered
> the face of the deep, while a wind from God swept over the
> face of the waters. Then God said, "Let there be light";
> and there was light. And God saw that the light was good;
> and God separated the light from the darkness...God saw
> everything that he had made, and indeed, it was very
> good.*
>
> GENESIS 1:1–4, 31

At the heart of the Christian doctrine of creation is the image of divine goodness and the goodness of the created world. The first moments of divine creativity and every succeeding moment reflect God's wisdom, intelligence, and love. With the psalmist, we can proclaim that "the heavens are telling the glory of God," but can we equally affirm that our digestive, cardiovascular, immune, and reproductive systems witness to God's glory? If we affirm that God's goodness creates our lives, then we must.

For those who affirm the doctrine of divine creation, there is no room for denial. In contrast to the ancient Gnostics, who saw the world as a prison house, and the contemporary new-age readers of *A Course in Miracles,* who state that "the world was not created by love," the biblical vision of creation affirms that this world in its entirety displays divine handiwork. Even human brokenness, reflected in substance abuse, eating disorders, obesity, and indifference to commonsense care for the body, cannot hide the essential fact of our existence that "you are the temple of God" and that "the body is the temple of God." Our basic state is original wholeness, a condition that shines through the deepest depression and disability for those who have eyes to see.

While many Christians have an uneasiness with embodiment, God revels in the world of bodies. God has created the color purple, the lilies of the valley, the raging sea, and the color of your hair. Along with the theologian Augustine, we Christians must affirm that whatever exists is inherently good. Only when we misuse God's good creation or love the created world *without* consideration of God's creativity do our bodies fall into sin and evil. This same world affirmation is proclaimed in the first chapter of John:

> In the beginning was the Word, and the Word was with God, and the Word was God. He was in the beginning with God. All things came into being through him, and without him not one thing came into being. What has come into being in him was life, and the life was the light of all people. The light shines in the darkness, and the darkness did not overcome it. (Jn. 1:1–5)

Anglican theologian William Temple once described Christianity as the world's most materialistic religion. God's creativity and love are celebrated in acts of embodiment. We see God's presence in the bread and wine of the eucharist, the fellowship of potluck dinners, the comfort of casseroles for those who grieve, the gentle waters of baptism, and the healing balm of the laying on of hands. Within the chaos of the world, God's goodness orders all things toward beauty and wholeness.

In the spirit of Orthodox Christianity, the doctrine of the goodness of creation affirms that all things are icons of God—windows through which God's providence and salvation are revealed. In a world in which "all things are works of God," to quote Hildegaard of Bingen, there are no God-forsaken places. In the words of the Jesuit poet Gerard Manley Hopkins, the world is charged with "God's grandeur, flaming out like shook foil."[3] In words that transcend gender, we can proclaim,

> This is my Father's world, and to my listening ears,
> all nature sings and round me rings the music of the spheres.
> This is my Father's world; I rest me in the thought
> of rocks and trees, of skies and seas; God's hands the wonders wrought.

> This is my Father's world; the birds their carols raise,
> the morning light, the flowers bright, declare their Maker's praise.
> Our God has made this world and he shines in all that's fair;
> in rustling grass I hear God pass, who speaks to me everywhere.

> MALTBIE D. BABCOCK, "THIS IS MY FATHER'S WORLD"

The Christian doctrine of creation is the foundation of the incarnation. Ultimately, all things—secular and religious—bear the imprint of God. Without the omnipresent embodiment of God in the essential goodness of the universe, the incarnation of Jesus Christ would be—as Gnostics ancient and modern suggest—purely a "rescue mission" from another sphere. Yet the goodness of creation is the womb from which the Savior is birthed. Without Mary's reproductive system, Jesus would never have been born. The light shines in the darkness of the womb as surely as it shines in the darkness of the heavens. The light of divine creation is also the light revealed in Jesus of Nazareth, whose gaze is turned earthward in healing love and acts of justice. "In Christ God was reconciling the world to himself" (2 Cor. 5:19). Christ is the "firstborn of all creation," the one in whom all things are united (Col. 1:15). With Matthew Fox, we must affirm that Christian theology is ultimately "creation theology" and that the goodness of the world always precedes the brokenness of sin. God's overflowing love takes flesh in Christ's redemption, but it also manifests itself in the light that shines in every cell and every creature.

The doctrine of divine creativity challenges us to love the world with the same intensity as God's. Although life involves destruction as well as creation and our survival demands the destruction of other living organisms, our attitude toward the nonhuman world should be characterized by reverence. With the first Americans, the doctrine of creation calls us to remember that "with beauty all around us, we walk." We affirm God's good creation by caring for the bodies—the whole person, the whole being—of others, both human and nonhuman.

At the intersection of our incarnation as whole persons and God's incarnation in the saving work of Christ, we embody the spirit of W. H. Auden's Christmas Oratorio, *For the Time Being:*

> He is the Way:
> Follow Him through the land of Unlikeness;
> You will see rare beasts and have unique adventures.

> He is the Truth.
> Seek him in the kingdom of Anxiety;
> You will come to a great city that has expected
> your return for years.

> He is the life.
> Love him in the World of the Flesh;
> And at your marriage all its occasions shall dance for joy.

EXERCISE ONE: LIVING BY YOUR AFFIRMATIONS

At the heart of the Christian doctrine of creation is the goodness of the world. Ultimately, this goodness must be affirmed in our own lives. There are numerous affirmations of divine goodness that concretize this experience of divine loving creativity. For example, we can affirm, "God's goodness creates *my life*," and then particularize that in affirmations such as: "God's goodness creates *my body*." "God's goodness creates *my sexuality*." "God's goodness creates *my imagination*."

In your own life, how would you concretize this affirmation? Take a few moments to experience God's goodness in the various aspects of your life. If all things are icons of God, then all human gifts and characteristics have their ultimate origin in the divine creativity.

God's goodness creates _____.
God's goodness creates _____.
God's goodness creates _____.
God's goodness creates _____.

Exercise Two: Living by Your Imagination

Once again, take time to be still and know that God is with you. Relax your body and let go of any stresses in your life today. In the quiet, begin to survey the universe, exploring whatever comes to mind in the macrocosmic world of planets and galaxies. As you gaze heavenward, experience the divine creative light permeating the planets and galaxies.

Move toward the microcosm. Ponder in the quiet your immediate environment, both natural and human-created. Experience the divine creative light permeating everything you consider.

Now, enter the world of animals. Experience the divine creative light permeating the chirping bird, the sleeping cat, the running dog. Turning to the human world, visualize certain persons who are near to you in spirit. Experience the divine creative light permeating their beings. Visualize a stranger or antagonist. Experience the divine creative light permeating their beings as well.

Now, turn to your own life. Experience the divine creative light permeating your mind, refreshing it with creative ideas. Experience the divine creative light permeating your body, flushing out toxins, washing away fatigue, enhancing the immune system. If there are any places of dis-ease or stress in your life—body, mind, or spirit—experience the divine creative light with its healing power embracing and permeating that part of your life.

Close with the affirmation "God's goodness creates my life and the life of all things."

Exercise Three: Faith in Action

Augustine proclaimed that whatever exists is good, inasmuch as it is created by God. In contrast to the new-age spiritual guidebook *A Course in Miracles'* pronouncement that "the body was not created by love," we affirm as Christians that the body was created by love. Body, mind, and spirit are equal manifestations of divine creativity. As members of the body of Christ, the universal community of God's children, we are called to "love God in the world of the flesh." We are called to be incarnational people who see the material world as pregnant with the divine spirit.

Our call as Christians is to bring forth the oft-hidden goodness of creation in others. This begins first with a vision of goodness in the other that is embodied, like God's incarnation in Christ, in loving acts toward neighbor and stranger.

This exercise has a number of components, both imaginative and active in nature. *First, commit yourself to seeing the goodness in others by affirming in every encounter with one of God's children that "God's goodness creates her or his life."* Be a spiritual detective, looking beneath the exterior to discover the true, holy reality of your neighbor or a stranger.

Second, discover ways that you can bring out the oft-hidden goodness in others. Look for their gifts and talents and—without being codependent or paternalistic/maternalistic—find ways to support their growth.

Third, commit yourself to appreciation of the value of the nonhuman world apart from your own human enjoyment. This commitment may manifest itself, first, in the study of the theology of ecology. Second, it may take shape in the willingness to change your eating habits (perhaps through eating less meat or poultry) and encourage in the economic order alternative means (range fed, range grazing) of raising poultry, beef, and pork. Third, commit yourself to nurturing beauty in your neighborhood and wider community. This can be manifested in attentiveness to litter in public places and parklands. It can also be manifested in a political commitment to protect the earth from undue human destruction. This may involve research on current building projects in your town or political action aimed at stopping the destruction of American wetlands and deserts by housing developments or the razing of the Amazon rain forests for cattle ranching.

Faith takes action when our visualizations of beauty become embodied in acts aimed at enhancing the beauty of the earth.

God Loves Me

> *For God so loved the world that he gave his only Son, so*
> *that everyone who believes in him may not perish but*
> *may have eternal life. Indeed, God did not send the Son*
> *into the world to condemn the world, but in order that the*
> *world might be saved through him.*
>
> JOHN 3:16–17

When Swiss theologian Karl Barth, the author of the compendious multivolume *Church Dogmatics,* was asked to describe the heart of Christian faith, he surprised his conversation partner by quoting from a children's hymn: "Jesus loves me this I know, for the Bible tells me so." Indeed, the heart of Christian theology is the love of God manifest in the life, ministry, death, and resurrection of Jesus of Nazareth. Beyond the theological descriptions of the divine nature and incarnation lies a simple truth: God loves you enough to share in your life and dwell in your heart. The apostle Paul proclaimed that "In Christ God was reconciling the world to himself" (2 Cor. 5:19). Although Christian theology has often been seduced by images of worldly power—the Caesar and the omnipotent king—in its description of God, the "Galilean vision" of divinity—the humble, suffering, intimate parent and companion—represents the unique contribution of Christianity to our understanding of God.

"For God so loved the world that he gave his only Son." Whatever else we say about the nature of Jesus as the Christ, the heart of the matter is familial love. The divine is fully present as the loving companion of humankind and the created world. The only God we can know as Christians is the God defined by Jesus' healing and loving presence in service to the one he called "Abba." Surely this is what the traditional doctrine of "fully human, fully divine" was trying to say—that is, that the universal love of God is fully manifested intimately and personally right where we are and in the presence of the humble Galilean teacher and healer we call Jesus.

The power, knowledge, and presence of God are ultimately defined by love. God's power is defined by God's aim at abundant life for all creation. God's knowledge reflects the intimate care of a parent. God's presence manifests the companionship, the "tender care that nothing ever be lost." The love of God redefines power in terms of relationship, healing, and transformation. It is nearer to us than we are to ourselves. In the words of Charles Wesley,

> Love divine, all loves excelling,
>   joy of heaven, to earth come down;
> fix in us thy humble dwelling, all thine faithful mercies crown;
> Jesus, thou art all compassion, pure, unbounded love thou art;
> visit us with thy salvation, enter every trembling heart.
>
> CHARLES WESLEY, "LOVE DIVINE, ALL LOVES EXCELLING"

While the despot and the feudal lord demand absolute obedience and punish any slight to their honor, God's love embraces the wayward son, the lost sheep, the misplaced coin. The doctrine of atonement proclaims God's unconditional love, reflected in God's willingness to share in our suffering that we might be saved. Atonement is not about restoring the honor of an arbitrary monarch, placating a hanging judge, or paying a cosmic debt on our behalf. It is about a homecoming feast— and a love that treats us as if we had not left at all. This is surely what the apostle Paul meant when he proclaimed, "While we still were sinners Christ died for us" (Rom. 5:8).

God is gracious to us. God gives us more than we deserve and redeems us even before we have turned away. The prodigal son was always home in his parents' hearts, but in his rebellion, he fled from their presence. The lost sheep was always surrounded by the shepherd's light, even when darkness was its only companion.

"While we still were sinners Christ died for us." The Divine Parent always takes the first, second, and third steps and always bears the pain of our unfaithfulness. No good parent, in spite of a child's behavior, would love her children *in spite of who they are.* Although some theologies speak as if God can barely tolerate a sinful humankind whose efforts are never good enough to satisfy divine perfection, I believe that the loving parent of Jesus Christ embraces our sin and shatteredness, even in its hideous forms, and transforms our sin through divine love. With Dietrich Bonhoeffer, we affirm that "only a suffering God can save us." The suffering God loves us *because we are God's own children—God's own creation.* "For God so loved the world that he gave his only Son." The cross is more than the substitutionary intervention of a distant God. It is the compassion and empathy of the God who has been with us all along. In the cross, our pain becomes God's pain, and God's pain transforms our narcissism into love for our wounded world.

O sacred Head, now wounded, with grief and shame weighed down;
now scornfully surrounded with thorns, thine only crown;
how pale thou art with anguish, with sore abuse and scorn!
How does that visage languish which once was bright as morn!

What thou, O Christ, hast suffered was all for sinners' gain:
mine, mine was the transgression, but thine the deadly pain.
Lo, here I fall, my Savior! 'Tis I deserve thy place;
look on me with thy favor, and keep me in thy grace.

What language shall I borrow to thank thee, dearest Friend,
for this thy dying sorrow, thy pity without end?
O make me thine forever; and should I fainting be,
O, let me never, never outlive my love to thee.

BERNARD OF CLAIRVAUX, "O SACRED HEAD, NOW WOUNDED"

While many Christians see John 3:16 as a statement of Christian exclusiveness, I believe that the statement invites us to experience God universally and inclusively as well as intimately and personally. "God so loved the world" is the heartbeat of God's universal providence. Our salvation does not depend on our adherence to orthodox creeds or performance of social action. Rather, God's salvation reaches out to each one of us regardless of our conscious relationship with Jesus Christ. Whatever healing and truth come from other religious traditions is grounded in God's omnipresent love for the world. This love is ubiquitous but not homogenous. A personal God also chooses to be present for us in a variety of ways, uniquely responding to each creature and culture. A personal God can also choose to reveal the divine nature to us more fully in certain situations and persons than in others. While we as Christians cannot limit God's presence to our tradition, we *can* affirm that Christ uniquely represents God's healing, saving, and transforming love for ourselves and for the planet.

The incarnation of Jesus of Nazareth is God's redemptive choice for us and for our salvation. But look again. This choice is for *all* creation. God's love extends to the nonhuman world that waits in eager longing for the fullness of salvation (Rom. 8:19). The love of God is also present in the "hidden Christ of India," the shaman of the Native Americans, and the Ancient Ones of Africa. God never is and has never been without a witness (Acts 14:17). As we recognize the universality of God's love, we are called to personally become incarnations of the spirit of Christ in our care for our brothers and sisters and for the nonhuman world.

EXERCISE ONE: LIVING BY YOUR AFFIRMATIONS

Today, we are called simply to affirm, "God loves me," or "Jesus loves me." When we let our imperfections stand between God and ourselves, we are reminded that by God's grace we are "clothed" in Christ and that God loves us with the same parental love that God had for Jesus of Nazareth our Savior. In this spirit, I affirm in my own life: "God loves me *regardless of my imperfections as a parent.*" "God loves me *regardless of my feelings of anger at the university administration.*" "God loves me *regardless of my fear of failure.*"

How would you concretize this affirmation in your life today?

God loves me _____.
God loves me _____.
God loves me _____.
God loves me _____.

EXERCISE TWO: LIVING BY YOUR IMAGINATION

In this visualization, once again take time to be still and be aware of your being in the presence of God. In the quiet, ponder any barriers that stand between you and God. These barriers can be past actions, attitudes, feelings of inadequacy, or guilt. Take a moment to experience the most significant barrier that stands between yourself and God. How does it feel? How does it keep you distant from God?

As you ponder the feelings that emerge, you realize that Jesus Christ is with you. Share the barriers with him. How does Jesus respond to your woundedness and alienation? In the quiet, hear Jesus speak words of love to you, "I love you _____. I accept and empower you just as you are." How does it feel to be the object of such unconditional love?

In conclusion, take a few minutes to thank God for his unconditional love for you. Thank God for the love of Jesus present in your own life today.

EXERCISE THREE: FAITH IN ACTION

In the first letter of John, the author describes the relationship between divine and human love:

Beloved, let us love one another, because love is from God; everyone who loves is born of God and knows God…God's love was revealed among us in this way: God sent God's only Son into the world so that we might live through him. In this is love, not that we loved God but that God loved us and sent God's Son to be the atoning sacrifice for our sins. Beloved, since God loved us so much, we also ought to love one another. No one has ever seen God; if we love one another, God lives in us, and God's love is perfected in us. (1 Jn. 4:7, 9–12)

By channeling God's love for us to our neighbor, we are awakened to God's presence in our lives.

Commit yourself today to see "only Christ" in every encounter. Treat each person as if he or she is a "little Christ," deserving of infinite care and compassion. When you are tempted to see the other as a nuisance, problem, or interruption, simply remind yourself to see her or him with God's eyes. Although you may still need to usher the person quickly out of the office or excuse yourself for the next meeting, it is not the quantity of time that you give the other that matters; it is the spirit of the encounter. Even if for only a second, give Christ's love to everyone you meet. Take the briefest of moments to pray for everyone you meet.

CHAPTER THREE

The Power of Christ and Creative Transformation

The Nicene Creed proclaims, "For us and our salvation Christ came down from heaven." While modern persons may struggle with the hierarchical, three-story universe and the nature of salvation characteristic of the fourth-century imagination and religious experience, Christian faith has historically identified the incarnation of God in Christ with the timeless quest for salvation and spiritual empowerment. To many persons, salvation is solely identified with eternal life. However, the biblical tradition has a broader understanding of salvation than merely disembodied spiritual existence. From the biblical perspective, salvation means *shalom*, the experience of wholeness of mind, body, spirit, relationships, and society. In this spirit, salvation also means deliverance from the forces of oppression, illness, and sin. Salvation is the continuous and universal process of transformation, always turning us from darkness to light, self-centeredness to community, and unbelief to faith. Ultimately, salvation involves the renewal, reformation, and re-creation of all aspects of our existence in this life, even as it stretches into eternity. A holistic, process-relational understanding of salvation, accordingly, includes what has been traditionally understood as *justification,* the experience of divine acceptance and forgiveness in the present moment, and *sanctification,* the ongoing experience of spiritual transformation over one's whole lifetime.

According to theologian John Cobb, Christ—the cosmic and personal principle of "creative transformation"—is found wherever the gift of "new creation" liberates us from our bondage to the past and the prison of self-imposed limitations. As in the days of the first century, Christ today calls us beyond the past toward the adventurous future of divine-human partnership and cocreativity. Those who follow Christ break down the walls of ethnic, social, and religious division, even as they break down the barriers of the past and their limitations.

For Christians, the embodiment of Christ is most present in Jesus of Nazareth—the teacher, healer, and revealer of the divine power of creative transformation. The incarnation goes well beyond issues of gynecology and miracles to embrace the fullness of our lives in all their grandeur and finitude.

The Light of the world, incarnate in Jesus of Nazareth, is also present as the inner light of all persons. Contrary to those who would limit Christ's saving presence to a particular denomination or faith tradition, God's revelation in Jesus Christ is abundant and ubiquitous in nature. The light shines in the darkness, but it also joins with God's other healing lights to illumine the world. Those who consciously live "in Christ" are challenged by Christ's power to "do even greater works" than the historical Jesus. With Christ as our deepest reality, we can—as the apostle Paul proclaims—"do all things."

Although Christian theology is Christ-centered theology, it also affirms that the journey toward self-discovery and divine discovery are one and the same. In the words of one church father, "the glory of God is a human being fully alive." It is my experience that as we become more fully alive in Christ, our lives become more dynamic, centered, synchronous, and creative. Narrow parochial boundaries give way to the affirmation of truth wherever it is experienced. We become "little Christs," the lively embodiments of divine love and creativity in our world.

In the affirmations of faith pertaining to the awareness of Christ's presence in our lives, we will explore the personal meaning of the incarnation as we experience Christ's empowerment in our lives. In discovering the personal meaning of the incarnation, we experience God's fullness in the most ordinary details of our everyday lives. God's aim is that we, like Jesus of Nazareth, "grow in wisdom and stature" and "attain the maturity of Christ" in our own lives. The reality of Christ is not far off but is a most intimate, growing, and changing reality, for the reign of God is within us and among us even today.

I Am a Child of God, Created in God's Image

> *Then God said, "Let us make humankind in our image,*
> *according to our likeness; and let them have dominion*
> *over the fish of the sea, and over the birds of the air, and*
> *over the cattle, and over all the wild animals of the earth,*
> *and over every creeping thing that creeps upon the earth."*
> *So God created humankind in his image, in the image of*
> *God he created them; male and female he created them.*
> *God blessed them.*
>
> GENESIS 1:26–28

The story is told of a young lion who came to live among goats. Imitating the goats around him, he ate grass like a goat and bleated like a goat. Though gigantic in stature, he was startled by the slightest noise. One day the great king of the jungle spotted the young lion among the herd of goats. As the lion king marched into the pasture, the goats scattered in fear. The young lion cowered before the king of the jungle, who proceeded to grab him by the mane and carry him to the nearby pond. "Look at your reflection," the great lion king roared, "You are a lion, not a goat; eat meat, roar, be fearless!"

Surely many of us have experienced life like the lion among goats. We have given up our power to determine our lives. We feel timid and weak, fearful of the boss's next remark or our spouse's next outburst. Our lives are often determined by external events to which we meekly react. We seldom initiate new behaviors for fear that they might upset the status quo and create conflict. Our inner voices tell us that we are unworthy of love and respect. We are the last in line for the abundant life and the last to be chosen for the children's games. We want to do the right thing, but we are held back by our fears.

Authentic Christianity begins with a very different self-image. A living christology begins with the creation of the universe. The Word that brings forth creation in the Genesis accounts is the same Word that John's gospel identifies as the light of the world. The wisdom that brought forth the universe is what gave birth to and inspired Jesus of Nazareth and also inspires us. From Christ's perspective, we are of infinite worth. Along with the whole universe, our lives are pronounced "good." We

75

are God's children. We are described—along with our Savior Jesus—as "the light of the world." We are created in God's image. We have not only the right to be here and but also the right to make our mark in the universe in partnership with our Creator and Companion.

Historically, there have been many attempts to describe what it means to be "created in God's image." This image has been identified with creativity, intelligence, reason, eternal life, and love. Yet because God and humankind are multidimensional, no one description can encompass what is meant by the "image of God" in humankind. What is more important than the details of specifying the image is recognizing that reality toward which the image points: The deepest dimension of humankind is God's presence in our lives. God's intimate presence ultimately defines our nature *and* our place in the universe. Beneath all the diverse expressions of the divine in human life is the one reality of God's spirit as the animating principle of each person's life.

I once participated in a spiritual growth exercise in which my partner kept asking, "Who are you?" Before I was eventually reduced to silence, I began with the obvious...Bruce Epperly...father...husband ...university professor and chaplain...walker...little league coach...American...male. Then, the more subtle definitions emerged...Christian...contemplative... seeker of God's shalom...child of God.

Who are you? You are ultimately a child of God, created in the divine image and constantly bathed in divine inspiration and affirmation. There is no room for self-deprecation among God's children. Each of us is unique in our own way, even as we radiate the presence of the divine parent in human life. Despite our failures and woundedness, God's imprint remains the defining characteristic around which our lives constellate. Beneath the often ambiguous lives we live, Christ's wholeness still shines forth and cannot be hidden. With the traditional Christmas hymn, we discover our holiness, even as we rejoice in God's presence in Jesus of Nazareth.

> Jesus is our childhood's pattern; day by day like us he grew,
> he was little, weak, and helpless, tears and smiles like us he knew.
> Thus he feels for all our sadness, and he shares in all our gladness.
>
> CECIL F. ALEXANDER, "ONCE IN ROYAL DAVID'S CITY"

Who are you? In contrast to those whose religious practices center around human sinfulness, the incarnation affirms first and foremost our original wholeness as God's beloved sons and daughters. In those sighs too deep for words, the spirit of Christ echoes the words given to Jesus at his baptism: "You are my beloved son in whom I am well pleased; you are my beloved daughter in whom I am well pleased." Human sin is significant precisely because it hides our true identities as God's children. Despite those who build walls of saved and unsaved, friend and foe, the fact is that you are a child of God, and so is your neighbor. Accordingly, I am called to claim the authority that God has given me and demand the respect of others. God calls us to creative self-affirmation. But just as important, I am called to claim the authority of God for my neighbor and demand that he or she also be treated with respect.

South African bishop Desmond Tutu spoke of Apartheid as Christian heresy, because it refused to recognize the holiness of persons of color. God's pronouncement of the divine image in humankind is unconditional and unlimited. The divine image is not determined by ethnicity, gender, intelligence, age, productivity, or medical condition.

At every stage of life, from conception to death, we are challenged to treasure the divine image. Although this recognition of the divine image does not give us absolute guidelines for the ethical issues surrounding life and death, it does counsel us always to aim at choosing life—affirming life's value and wholeness—regardless of the cultural norms within which we may live. We are called especially to choose life for the children—to bathe them in affirmations and love, to guide them in experiencing God's calling for their lives, and to defend them from all kinds of personal, economic, psychological, sexual, and theological abuse. In the hymn "Strong, Gentle Children," we hear God's voice calling us to cherish God's image in our own inner child and in the children in our midst.

> Strong, gentle children, God made you beautiful,
> gave you the wisdom and power you need;
> speak in the stillness all you are longing for;
> live out your calling to love and to lead.
>
> Strong, hurting children, angry and terrified,
> open the secrets your life has concealed;
> though you are wounded, know you are not to blame;
> cry out your story till truth is revealed.
>
> Strong, knowing children, utter your cry aloud,
> honor the wisdom God gave you at birth;
> speak to your elders till they have heard your voice;
> sing out your vision of healing on earth.
>
> DAN DAMON, "STRONG, GENTLE CHILDREN"

The divine image within is the ultimate, nonnegotiable affirmation of our lives. It proclaims our value, worth, and significance as objects of divine love and inspiration. Today, our human self-affirmation must go beyond the traditional affirmation of our personhood and our species. The vision of the "beloved community," articulated by Martin Luther King, Jr., challenges us to see holiness in all things, even in the nonhuman world. Even when we make judgments of value based on the needs of our species, we still are reminded to honor and cherish God's other "created" children and live in gratitude for their gift of life to us.

Who are you? You are a child of God. You are like Jesus Christ: God's beloved son, God's beloved daughter. This is the heart of the atonement, the at-one-ment that unites with their creator those who thought themselves alone and alienated. Stand tall, roar like the Christ-lion Aslan, and claim your power for holy partnership with God and your neighbor. Claim the divine image, the "Christ in you, the hope of glory" (Col. 1:27).

EXERCISE ONE: LIVING BY YOUR AFFIRMATIONS

For your affirmation regularly repeat, "I am a child of God, created in God's image." Whenever you feel your self-confidence or self-worth fading, reaffirm, "I am a child of God, created in God's image" as an antidote to feelings of powerlessness and low self-esteem.

Try to connect this divinely given self-affirmation with the concrete events of your life. In so doing, you will be able to connect the twin poles of being and doing, self-affirmation and creative activity. For example, I affirm in my own life: "I am a child of God; *I respect myself.*" "I am created in God's image; *I have the resources to solve this problem.*" "I am a child of God; *I am loved and I love others.*" "I am created in God's image; *I can succeed in this new endeavor.*" "I am a child of God; *I deserve justice and respect.*" "I am a child of God; *I can do great things in my life.*"

In your own life, take time to concretize these affirmations by connecting them with issues you are currently facing.

I am a child of God; _____.
I am created in God's image; _____.
I am a child of God; _____.
I am created in God's image; _____.

EXERCISE TWO: LIVING BY YOUR IMAGINATION

There is a close connection between image and imagination. Indeed, through holy imagination, the dynamic image of God, the Christ within, takes flesh in our own lives. A story is told of the sculptor Michelangelo. One day a curious neighbor observed him rolling a boulder up the street and onto his porch. The neighbor was overcome with curiosity when Michelangelo began to pound on the boulder with his chisel. "Why are you pounding this boulder?" he asked. To which Michelangelo replied, "There's an angel inside, and I'm trying to let it out!" Spiritual formation is grounded in bringing forth the angelic and holy in ourselves and others.

Take some time to relax in stillness. Visualize your own life in terms of a boulder. Explore the boulder in terms of its hardness and coldness. What does the boulder look like? What is its shape? What aspects of the boulder hide your true nature? What aspects imprison the divine presence in your life? What aspects of the boulder hurt you as they hurt others?

As you meditate on the hidden divinity of your life, you hear a pounding sound. Jesus is pounding on the boulder, breaking loose the unnecessary encapsulation of your potential, bringing forth the holiness within your life. Visualize your holiness slowly emerging. Visualize the Christ light within you bursting forth. What does it feel like to have your divine image emerge from the boulder? What shape is it taking? What is it like to have your divine image come forth as it is meant to be?

In your gratitude for Christ's liberation of the divine image within your own life, your field of awareness is broadened as you notice another boulder nearby. Who is hidden in that boulder? What things—to the best of your knowledge—prevent you from seeing the divine image in that boulder? What things prevent that boulder from experiencing itself as a manifestation of the divine image? What can you do to bring the angelic forth from that rough-hewn rock? Take some time to assist in freeing the divine image of this hidden angel from its imprisonment.

Conclude by joyfully embracing yourself and the other as you affirm the image of God in your lives.

EXERCISE THREE: FAITH IN ACTION

Mother Teresa of Calcutta committed herself to seeing God in all the hideous disguises among the poor, sick, and dying. We live in a world that often defaces the divine image. We focus on the "boulder" of ethnicity, religion, intelligence, appearance, economics, gender, or sexual orientation, blinding ourselves to the angelic within. As you explore the boulders in your own community, what actions can you take to transcend the "us versus them" attitudes so prevalent in our time? How can you overcome the polarizations of pro-life and pro-choice, homosexual and heterosexual, Christian and Muslim?

Created in the image of God, we are challenged to speak the truth with love to all we meet. Accordingly, make a commitment to seek out the image of God, even in your enemies. While it is easy to demonize Saddam Hussein, the Littleton killers, survivalists, and creation scientists, we can also build a bridge of human affirmation that focuses on common concerns. The point is not conversion or agreement with the other, but loving affirmation based on God's love for and presence within all of us. Guard your tongue, so that you speak with respect even of your opponent. Like the fabled Luke Skywalker, look for the good even in the diabolical Darth Vaders of your life. When we surround our neighbors with loving-kindness, their hearts may open to the divine intention for their lives. Further, unless you discover the divine image in your neighbor, the divine image in your own life will elude you.

We are called to speak and see the truth of the image of God in each person. As Christians, we can learn something from an ancient Hindu greeting. When two persons meet in India, it is customary that they fold their hands together prayerfully and greet each other with the word *Namaste*, which is roughly translated, "I honor the divine presence in you." A Christian variation on this greeting might be "The Spirit in me greets the Spirit in you" or "The Christ in me greets the Christ in you." Such greetings, similar to the initial meaning of "Hello" or "Health to you," are spoken reminders of the fact that we are always on holy ground as the "I" greets the "Thou." Take time in even the most ordinary greetings to address the divine presence in your neighbor and the stranger.

I Am an Inspired Child of God

Now the word of the LORD came to me saying, "Before I formed you in the womb I knew you, and before you were born I consecrated you; I appointed you a prophet to the nations." Then I said, "Ah, Lord GOD! Truly I do not know how to speak, for I am only a boy." But the LORD said to me, "Do not say, 'I am only a boy'; for you shall go to all to whom I send you, and you shall speak whatever I command you. Do not be afraid of them, for I am with you to deliver you, says the LORD."

JEREMIAH 1:4–8

Biblical Christianity proclaims that all persons have a vocation or calling that arises from God's presence in their lives. While God's plan is always concrete and constantly adjusting itself to respond to the needs of the world, within each person's life are many gifts and tendencies whose purpose is to contribute to the healing and transformation of the world.

Like the sculptor Michelangelo's discovery of angels in boulders, God's vision of your gifts often reveals something in your life that was previously hidden from you. This imaginative vision was at the heart of Christ's ministry: Jesus saw a loyal disciple in a hated tax collector, a spiritual rock in the vacillating Peter, a spiritual teacher in a prostitute, a global missionary in the doubting Thomas. Christ sees a person of power and beauty in you!

When God calls Jeremiah to become his prophet in a wayward land, he reveals to Jeremiah talents and gifts that this young man had never imagined. "Before I formed you in the womb I knew you; and before you were born I consecrated you." This is not an impersonal pre-destination, but a personal calling that brings together God's gifts and Jeremiah's freedom.

At first, Jeremiah's freedom is expressed solely in his denial of his calling. "I am too young to speak to the elders. I am not articulate enough to command their respect and attention."

In reply, God reminds him that the Giver of his gifts will bring these gifts to their completion in his life. "Do not be afraid, Jeremiah. I am

81

with you always. Listen to my voice and you will know what to say to the elders. From now on, you are speaking for me, and I will be speaking through you."

Have you ever thought that you were inspired by God and that God might be revealing divine truth through your life? While such an affirmation may seem grandiose, this is precisely what the providence of God means in terms of the guidance we receive. God is constantly presenting us with new and innovative possibilities through insight, intuitive hunches, creative ideas, and dreams, as well as synchronous encounters. As the apostle Paul affirms, the Spirit of God constantly speaks to us "in sighs too deep for words." There are no gaps in God's inspiration. There are only failures to experience and act upon the presence of God in our lives. When Jesus asserts that "I stand at the door and knock," this is not a one-time, dramatic call to conversion, but a ubiquitous, recurring, many-faceted invitation to turn to God in each moment of our lives. The story is told of an ambitious evangelical student who accosted Professor Hal Luccock as he strolled across Yale's green. "Are you saved?" the young evangelist asked. "Yes, I am," responded the professor. "I am saved every day." Although there are decisive moments of inspiration, divine wisdom comes to us every millisecond, adjusting itself to our lives and the universe, calling us to our true vocation, that place where our gifts meet the world's needs.

Our lives are our gifts to God and our neighbors. God is best praised when we incarnate the divine inspiration as it flows through us toward our neighbor. As we commit our gifts to God, we become channels of God's abundant care for our world. In the spirit of the hymn "Take My Life," our lives and actions become ceaseless praise to the Spirit inspiring us all.

> Take my life, and let it be consecrated, Lord, to thee.
> Take my moments and my days; let them flow in ceaseless praise…
> Take my hands, and let them move at the impulse of thy love.
> Take my feet, and let them be swift and beautiful for thee…
>
> Take my voice, and let me sing; unto God my praise I bring.
> Take my lips and let them be filled with messages from thee…
> Take my silver and my gold, not a mite would I withhold;
> Take my intellect, and use every power as thou shalt choose.
>
>   FRANCES R. HAVERGAL, "TAKE MY LIFE"

God's counsel to Jeremiah is also meant for us whenever we perceive that our inexperience or imperfection might stand in the way of God's call in our lives. "Do not say you are only a child!" Nothing disqualifies us from becoming God's voice for love, truth, and healing. In our moments of doubt and low self-esteem, God challenges us with the affirmation "Yes, you can; yes, you can," until we discover for ourselves our own personal affirmation, "Yes, I can; yes, I can." God reminds us that life flourishes by our affirmations. While the poverty thinker lives by the "I am not," those who hear God's voice proclaim, "By God's grace, I am the one."

Biblical scholar Walter Brueggemann notes that the heart of the prophetic vision was the prophet's presentation of alternative reality, a different way of seeing the social and economic life of the nation. In the calling of virtually every prophet, the prophet had to embrace, first of all, God's alternative vision of himself or herself. As we look at our own lives, what alternative vision of ourselves is God giving us today? What self-imposed limitations is God breaking down so that we might experience the true joys of discipleship? What negative self-images need to be broken so that we might truly come to see ourselves as God sees us? The Christ within calls us forward, always with a vision of service, always with the promise "I am with you. Yes, you can!"

EXERCISE ONE: LIVING BY YOUR AFFIRMATIONS

Once again, we will live with two affirmations: "I am an inspired child of God," and "God speaks through my life and words." In my own life, I personalize these affirmations in the following manner: "I am an inspired child of God; *God is guiding my life toward fulfillment for myself and others.*" "God speaks through my life and words; *God speaks as I preach today.*" "I am an inspired child of God; *good ideas are constantly coming to me in my speaking and writing.*" "God speaks through my life and words; *God is giving me the right thing to say in this situation.*"

In your own life, take time to personalize these affirmations in a way that relates to what you are experiencing.

God speaks through my life and words; _____.
I am an inspired child of God; _____.
God speaks through my life and words; _____.
I am an inspired child of God; _____.

EXERCISE TWO: LIVING BY YOUR IMAGINATION

Quietly calm your body, mind, and spirit as you reflect on the story of Jeremiah. As you look at your life, what gifts and talents do you possess that can be utilized for the well-being of others? Visualize each gift and the place where it will be most needed.What are your fears in relationship to exploring these gifts?

As your ponder the polarity of vocation and fear, you hear the voice of God. "Before you were born, I knew you. Before you were born, I consecrated you. I will be with you to deliver you. I will show you what to say and do." How do you feel as you hear the voice of God? What gift is God calling forth in your life today? Experience the courage that comes from knowing that God will be with you as you explore your gifts for service.

EXERCISE THREE: FAITH IN ACTION

This exercise integrates the inner and outer journeys. Ponder a situation in which you are called to embody an alternative reality. Trusting God's presence, commit yourself to transcending your fears and letting God speak through you. As you speak your alternative word, listen to the guidance of the "still, small voice within you." How does God's voice speak through conflicts that emerge when we share our experiences of the divine?

Observe the life of another, possibly a child. Observe her or his gifts and talents as they present themselves to you. Pray that the person realizes his or her gifts. Speak words of encouragement that enable her or him to have confidence in the gifts. Help the person see the gifts that may previously have been overlooked.

I Am the Light of the World

*You are the light of the world. A city built on a hill cannot
be hid. No one after lighting a lamp puts it under the
bushel basket, but on the lampstand, and it gives light to
all in the house. In the same way, let your light shine
before others, so that they may see your good works and
give glory to your Father in heaven.*

MATTHEW 5:14–16

*All things came into being through him, and without him
not one thing came into being. What has come into being
in him was life, and the life was the light of all people.
The light shines in the darkness, and the darkness did not
overcome it...The true light, which enlightens everyone,
was coming into the world.*

JOHN 1:3–5, 9

The prologue to John's gospel joins christology, soteriology, and anthropology. The creative light of Christ is the source of our salvation, healing, and inspiration. The light of Christ enlightens everyone. Christ's influence is universal as well as individual. As the incarnation of God in all things, Christ is also the circle whose center of light is everywhere and whose circumference is nowhere. No darkness of flesh or spirit can ultimately triumph over the light of the world.

As followers of Christ, we are also manifestations of the incarnation. We are concrete words of God in our world. Christ affirms that his saving and healing light is present in our inner lights and external gifts— "You are the light of the world." Whereas Christ's disciples consciously claim the light that is their legacy, all persons are potential revealers of the divine light.

When Jesus proclaims, "You are the light of the world," his words challenge any feelings of godforsakenness or unworthiness we might harbor about ourselves. Your essence is light, love, and creativity. The darkness within or around you can never ultimately constrict the divine light that enlivens your life.

To claim consciously your identity as "the light of the world" is to recognize that the light within you is meant for service as well as personal fulfillment. "Let your light shine before others, so that they may see your good works and give glory to your Father in heaven." Our identities are the ground of our vocation as channels of the divine light we have received. Our light is also meant to shine in the darkness. When we join the light of Christ in our lives with that same light in others, the darkness of the world can never conquer it. In letting our lights shine, we share the guidance, insight, and enlightenment we have received. In affirming our own brightly shining and radiating light, we call forth the light in others. This is the divine abundance that confounds all "zero sum," bottom-line thinking. For in God's world, our light shines more brightly as we share it with others. Jim Strathdee's rendition of a Howard Thurman poem invites us to become God's light in the world through acts of justice and reconciliation.

> "I am the light of the world! You people come and follow me!"
> If you follow and love you'll learn the mystery
> of what you were meant to do and be.
>
> When the song of the angels is stilled,
> when the star in the sky is gone,
> when the magi and shepherds have found their way home,
> the work of Christmas is begun.
>
> To find the lost and lonely one,
> to heal the broken soul with love,
> to feed the hungry children with warmth and good food,
> to feel the earth below, the sky above!
>
> To free the pris'ner from all chains,
> to make the powerful care,
> to rebuild the nations with strength of good will,
> to see God's children ev'rywhere!
>
> To bring hope to ev'ry task you do,
> to dance at a baby's new birth,
> to make music in an old person's heart,
> and sing to the colors of the earth!
>
> "I am the light of the world! You people come and follow me."
> If you follow and love you'll learn the mystery
> of what you were meant to do and be.
>
> JIM STRATHDEE, "I AM THE LIGHT OF THE WORLD"

Who are you? Beyond all your fears and surface identities, you are the light of the world. You are God's beloved child. You are God's delight and Christ's partner in re-creating the universe. Dance in the light, and let the light shine wherever you are.

EXERCISE ONE: LIVING BY YOUR AFFIRMATIONS

As you embody this affirmation, simply repeat the phrase "I am the light of the world." In certain situations, you may choose a more active affirmation such as "God's light shines through me" or "I am the light of the world in this situation."

In concretizing this affirmation, I have adapted it to fit my own daily life: "I am the light of the world; *I share God's light in this lecture (or sermon)*." "God's light shines through me to *dispel the anger in this situation*." "I am the light of the world; *I bring light and wisdom to this meeting*." "God's light shines through me to *bring healing to this person*."

In what ways do you need to open to the presence of God's light in your life?

I am the light of the world; _____.
God's light shines through me to _____.
I am the light of the world; _____.
God's light shines through me to _____.

EXERCISE TWO: LIVING BY YOUR IMAGINATION

Twentieth-century African American mystic Howard Thurman tells of growing up in rural Florida. One hot summer day, young Howard went on a berry picking expedition. He plunged through the woods, filling his pail and his mouth with the crimson berries. Heedless of space or time, he went from bush to bush in search of the sweet, juicy berries. Without warning, young Howard heard the crash of thunder, signaling that a storm was approaching. He looked around and discovered that he was lost. As the sky darkened and raindrops began to fall, he began to panic. Resisting the urge to run aimlessly through the woods, he chose to stand completely still. The lightning frightened him, but each flash also illuminated the woods for a brief moment. Young Howard waited quietly and attentively. With each lightning strike, he looked in a different direction. Eventually, he saw something familiar. With each succeeding strike, he wended his way closer to home. For those who are patient, there is a guiding light even in the deepest darkness.

In the spirit of Howard Thurman's adventure, visualize yourself lost in a deep, dark woodland. You have strayed off the path and can find no familiar landmarks. As you gaze into the pitch blackness of the forest, what looms ahead in the darkness? What unseen threats lurk in the darkness? Visualize these threats.

Yet in the darkness, you remember your own inner light. Visualize it shining forth and the darkness becoming illuminated. You begin to see some familiar landmarks on your path. Note how it feels to be illuminated by the light.

In the distance, you see another pilgrim. That pilgrim is—like you were a few moments ago—lost and anxious. As you come near him, let your light shine forth to illuminate this pilgrim's way. As you travel together, now sure of your destination, you see a greater light in the distance, the light of Christ, that illumines the path you are on brighter than any light you have seen before.

Conclude your visualization by committing yourself to seeing the light in all situations and bringing it forth in others. Thank God for the light of Christ within your life.

EXERCISE THREE: FAITH IN ACTION

At the heart of the gospel of Matthew's portrayal of the light of the world is the recognition that we are lights for one another. We are called to see and bring forth the light of God in our neighbor's life even as we awaken to God's light in our own life. In the spirit of "letting your light shine," reflect on some part of your world in which the forces of light and darkness contend with one another. This may be a troubled family, a poorly operating elementary school, a conflict-ridden church, or the overall violence and injustice in our society.

As you reflect on these grim and chaotic realities of our lives, commit yourself to being a child of light. In every situation, imagine your light shining on those around you. Imagine the light of Christ emanating from everyone you meet. Reflect on how you—as a light bearer—can bring light to a chaotic world. Commit yourself to loving action that supports the social infrastructures that are necessary for the divine light to be noticed. Find a specific situation or person for whom your light may shine. Imagine them surrounded by the divine light. Do all that is appropriate to bring forth that light in the structures of our society with which you are familiar and the experiences of individuals whom you know.

I Can Do All Things through Christ Who Strengthens Me

I have learned to be content with whatever I have. I know what it is to have little, and I know what it is to have plenty. In any and all circumstances I have learned the secret of being well-fed and of going hungry, of having plenty and of being in need. I can do all things through him who strengthens me.

PHILIPPIANS 4:11b–13

"The glory of God is a human fully alive." At the heart of christology is God's desire that humankind have the abundant life that comes from our alignment with God's plan for each person's life. Jesus' entire ministry was oriented toward wholeness and growth of mind, body, spirit, and relationship. Jesus called persons to greatness and provided the insight and power to achieve what they had previously thought was impossible. God is on your side, and God will supply your needs.

The reality of our lives is that we seldom claim the stature of Christlikeness. At the slightest failure, our spirits shrink and our confidence in God disappears. We forget God's presence in our previous successess and failures. In such moments, we need to claim the biblical promise of Emmanuel, "God with us." We need to claim Paul's counsel to "be content with whatever I have," not as an excuse for passivity, but as an invitation to become alert to the divine possibilities present within failure and conflict. We need to see our lives from the perspective of God's plan for us and not from the vantage point of one discrete event.

In *The Alchemist,* Paulo Coehlo speaks of life's adventure in terms of realizing one's own personal legend. I believe that this insight is also at the heart of Paul's affirmation "I can do all things through Christ who strengthens me." Jesus Christ comes to us not so much as a heavenly person to be worshiped, but as the source of an intimate dream to follow. Conforming to Christ means living out your own personal, divinely inspired dreams in light of Christ's all-embracing, all-supporting love and guidance. When we follow Christ's personal dreams for us, revealed in each moment of our lives, we grow in vitality and stature. Although I

89

do not believe that we are puppets in the hands of God, I believe that even within our failures God invites us to a more dynamic spirituality.

But to claim "I can do all things" does not imply that one will "leap tall buildings in a single bound" or fly "faster than a locomotive." Along with Augustine, I recognize that the "miracles" God has planned for us are not violations of our nature and gifts, but deeper expressions of what we are meant to be. The divine promise is that when we place our lives in God's hands and align our dreams with God's vision for us, we will actualize concretely our unique gifts for ourselves and the world. Through Christ, we can do everything we need to succeed, prosper, and serve God. Jesus promised that we can do "greater things" even than he did for our well-being and our neighbor's.

Many biblical stories are about the fulfillment of this promise of abundant life and personal triumph: In the battle of David and Goliath, in the miracle of the loaves and fishes, the wedding feast at Cana, and in the friends of the paralyzed man, God presents persons with both a dream and the means to achieve it. Even in the most challenging situations, God will provide the resources, power, guidance, and insight for us to live the abundant life here and now. God always leads us toward our own personal legend and then challenges us to go beyond all self-imposed barriers.

In my own daily walking prayer, I have customized this affirmation to suit my own spiritual and emotional needs and gifts. In my early-morning aerobic walk through the woods behind our home, I ruminate on God's presence in my life, using the affirmation "I can do all things through Christ who stregthens me. I am a powerhouse." The same energy that created the universe is flowing through me. The divine power, the *chi* energy of Chinese philosophy, that flowed from Jesus to those he healed is coursing through my mind and body. Aligned with Christ, I am a powerhouse and wellspring of creative ideas and have the resources to put them into practice. In every situation, I am a channel of divine energy and blessing. When we would complain that no one is here to help us, Jesus challenges us, as he challenged the man at the pool, with the affirmation "I am here. Stand up. Take up your bed and walk." If God is on our side, then we will be able to live creatively and powerfully regardless of life's situations. We can face illness with grace and courage and conflict with sensitivity and strength. We can confront our own personal demons and know that God will see us through. As powerhouses for God's reconciliation and grace, we can sing with Harry Emerson Fosdick:

God of grace and God of glory,
on thy people pour thy power;
crown thine ancient church's story;
bring its bud to glorious flower.
Grant us wisdom, grant us courage,
for the facing of this hour...

Lo! the hosts of evil round us
scorn thy Christ, assail thy ways!
From the fears that long have bound us,
free our hearts to faith and praise.
Grant us wisdom, grant us courage,
for the living of these days...

Set our feet on lofty places;
fill our lives that we may be
strengthened with all Christ-like graces
pledged to set all captives free.
Grant us wisdom, grant us courage,
lest we fail our call from thee.

HARRY EMERSON FOSDICK, "GOD OF GRACE AND GOD OF GLORY"

EXERCISE ONE: LIVING BY YOUR AFFIRMATIONS

In alignment with the discipline of spiritual formation we are developing, take time through the day to repeat this simple affirmation or a variation of it: "I can do all things through Christ who strengthens me."

To concretize this affirmation, expand it to relate to your current life situation. In times of uncertainty or fear, use this affirmation as a shield against the darkness. Remember always that Christ is strengthening you, especially when you feel most vulnerable. In my own life, I have concretized this affirmation by repeating, "I can do all things through Christ who strengthens me; *God is empowering me in this situation.*" "I can do all things through Christ who strengthens me; *I have resources to speak the truth with love in this conflict.*" "I can do all things through Christ who strengthens me; *God is giving me wisdom and insight for this meeting.*"

In your own life, concretize this affirmation in a way that is uniquely personal for you:

I can do all things through Christ who strengthens me;

_____.

I can do all things through Christ who strengthens me;
_____.

I can do all things through Christ who strengthens me;
_____.

I can do all things through Christ who strengthens me;
_____.

EXERCISE TWO: LIVING BY YOUR IMAGINATION

In quiet reflection, look at your life today. What are your dreams? What vision are you meant to live out in order to fulfill yourself and heal your world? As you ponder your vision, what obstacles are standing in the way of its embodiment in your life?

As you reflect on the obstacles, visualize the presence of Christ alongside you. Experience God's energy flowing through your life. Experience God's inner strength giving you the power to overcome these obstacles. Begin to look at your dreams one by one. With Christ as your partner, see yourself as a cocreator with Christ in bringing forth each of these dreams for yourself and the world. (You may use this meditation for each dream or for your overall "personal legend" as you currently understand it.)

Conclude your visualization by giving thanks for the dreams and gifts that God has given you and the divine power that is enabling you to manifest these gifts and dreams in your life.

EXERCISE THREE: FAITH IN ACTION

Our gifts are intended for service. Within the body of Christ, each person has a unique gift to contribute. Reflect on the interplay of your gifts and the world's needs. Experience the power that Christ is giving you flowing within your life and toward another person, enabling that person to realize her or his own deepest gifts.

In this spirit, commit yourself to sharing these gifts with persons in need of care and empowerment. As a channel of the divine energy, you may feel called to the holy work of visiting an elderly shut-in, volunteering at a soup kitchen, or perhaps tutoring an underprivileged child.

Recognizing the power of the word to shape our lives and perceptions of reality, explore the language that you use. Is your self-talk oriented toward achievement and service? Do your words and thoughts about others contribute to their well-being? With conscious awareness of your language, commit yourself to speaking only words of affirmation and love. Even when you must challenge a particular behavior, commit yourself to making your comments edifying and life-enhancing. Let your every word be aimed at reconciliation and encouragement of those with whom you interact.

I Am Strong in the Lord

> The LORD is my strength and my shield;
>   in him my heart trusts;
> so I am helped, and my heart exults,
>   and with my song I give thanks to him.
> The LORD is the strength of his people;
>   he is the saving refuge of his anointed.
> O save your people, and bless your heritage;
>   be their shepherd, and carry them forever.
>
> PSALM 28:7–9

What does it mean to be a strong person? In popular culture and the business world, strength is often identified with the fearless stoicism of a John Wayne, the laser-like competitiveness of a Bill Gates, or the stamina and resourcefulness of a Navy Seal. The strength of a nation is often defined in terms of its military might and nuclear arsenal. Although these are popular measures of strength, the biblical tradition presents an alternative vision of strength: the relational power and mutuality that come from alignment with God's presence in one's life. A person of strength is a person of stature, one who is not afraid to embrace and integrate diverse and contrasting experiences and persons. In Chinese philosophy, strength is often identified with the *Tao,* the gentle power that undergirds and nurtures all things. Whereas the inflexible oak tree crashes down in the storms of life, the flexible, interdependent bamboo remains standing. God's power is made perfect in what the world often perceives as weakness. The way of the cross is ironically the way of wholeness and transformation.

The biblical tradition roots one's personal strength in the ability to trust God in difficult situations. Its vitality lies in the faith that the One who has begun working in our lives will not rest until our lives reach wholeness. By this lively confidence in God, our lives become rooted in the resources of a power beyond and within ourselves. The gentle, unconquered power of the universe flows in and through us.

Strength and courage are a matter of trust and perspective. When the Israelite spies were sent into Canaan, the majority report was that Israel had no chance to defeat Canaan's inhabitants. "We are not able to go up against this people, for they are stronger than we," reported the spies. "The land that we have gone through as spies is a land that devours its inhabitants; and all the people that we saw in it are of great size. There we saw the Nephilim...and to ourselves we seemed like grasshoppers, and so we seemed to them." Only Joshua and Caleb trusted the unseen promises of God. From the eyes of faith, they saw victory instead of defeat: "The land that we went through as spies is an exceedingly good land. If the LORD is pleased with us, he will bring us into this land and give it to us, a land that flows with milk and honey...the LORD is with us; do not fear them" (Num. 13:31–34; 14:7b–9). Centuries later, when Goliath boasted of his strength, the Israelites quaked in fear, while David alone claimed the strength of God's promise to the people.

Although these military metaphors may not be applicable to our lives, it is clear that we all must face what the American philosopher/ psychologist William James described as "the moral equivalent of war"— the definitive event that challenges our faith in ourselves and in God and calls forth all our inner resources in the contest for truth, beauty, and justice. This moral equivalent of war was present in Gandhi's pacifist struggle for India's self-rule, Martin Luther King, Jr.'s, willingness to suffer injustice so that the oppressor might be transformed, and Dorothy Day's quest for justice for the poor of the city. The moral equivalent of war is present in our own lives when we face the powers of darkness, fear, hatred, and injustice in ourselves and in the world and, despite our insecurities and anxieties about conflict, continue to choose the path of life. In such conflicts, our power finds its source in the One whose energy and guidance grounds and inspires our lives. Rooted in God's love, we can be "victors in the midst of strife" as we sing with the crusaders for peace and justice:

> We shall overcome, we shall overcome,
> we shall overcome someday!
> Oh, deep in my heart I do believe
> we shall overcome someday!

> The Lord will see us through, the Lord will see us through,
> the Lord will see us through someday!

> We'll walk hand in hand, we'll walk hand in hand,
> we'll walk hand in hand someday!

> We are not afraid, we are not afraid,
> we are not afraid today!

The truth shall make us free, the truth shall make us free,
the truth shall make us free someday!

We shall live in peace, we shall live in peace,
we shall live in peace someday!
Deep in my heart, I do believe
we shall overcome someday!

AFRICAN AMERICAN SPIRITUAL, "WE SHALL OVERCOME"

Each day we see the strength of God incarnate in the lives of persons who are facing adversity and yet go forth in the power of God's presence. We see it in the widow who picks up the pieces of her shattered life, faces the loneliness of life without her husband of five decades, and invests her deep love for him in a new direction—volunteer work at a nursing home. We see it in the inner-city children whose pilgrimages to school take them through a maze of drug--infested neighborhoods, but refuse to be conformed to the ways of death that confront them daily. Against the pressure of peers and the intimidation of drug dealers and gang members, they choose academic excellence and moral centeredness. We see it in the young man with severe depression who gets up each morning and commits himself to face the challenges of his disease in pursuit of his doctoral degree. We see it in ourselves when we follow our deepest dreams despite all the impediments that stand in our way. This is hope in the unseen, and in the unseen force that lures us forward is the unobtrusive energy that creates the universe and gives life to each cell.

We are strong in the Lord. Grounded in God, we find courage amid conflict, and power amid insecurity. Focused on Christ's presence in our lives, we can defy all the negative voices in our lives and in those around us. When Peter saw Christ walking on the water, he rushed out to meet him. As long as he focused on Jesus, Peter could do the impossible. But when he allowed the wind and waves to determine his reality, he sunk helplessly into the sea. As we examine our own lives, is our deepest personal reality the ever-resourceful, constantly innovative Christ within, or is it the fear that binds us? Is Christ our primary focus amid the challenges of life, or do we depend on material things or personal successes for our ultimate support? Do we focus on Christ as the source of our strength and inspiration?

This same groundedness in God is at the heart of the social and personal message of Psalm 28. The Psalm speaks of the authentic strength of the country that trusts in God. From the perspective of Psalm 28, what often passes for national strength—nuclear weapons, fighter planes, biological and chemical devices, antiballistic missile systems—is ironically a sign of weakness and a failure to recognize the true priorities of a nation-state—justice for all persons, care for the helpless, peaceful relations with its neighbors. Further, the reliance on force ultimately places our lives at greater risk from hair-trigger nuclear weapons and irrational terrorists. In the spirit of *Tao,* the greatest of states may be the one that seeks to be an instrument of peace, that beats swords into plowshares and tanks into playground equipment. Violence is contagious, but so is peace. As people discover the protection and strength in God's presence in their lives, the witness of their own lives will bring peace to their children, spouses, neighbors, and communities.

The power of love dwarfs every power known to humankind. The way of the cross is the way of victory for every segment of humankind. Regardless of what happens to us, when we are rooted in God, we are strong. As Paul proclaims in Romans 8:37, "In all these things we are more than conquerors." Our victory becomes the victory of all persons as our circle of power finds its strength in the divine circle encompassing all things.

EXERCISE ONE: LIVING BY YOUR AFFIRMATIONS

In this exercise, simply affirm on a regular basis: "I am strong in the Lord; I am strong in the Lord; I am strong in the Lord," as you experience a divine strength pouring into your life.

To concretize this, relate the affirmation to a situation in your life. In my own life, I have affirmed: "I am strong in the Lord; God's strength empowers me as I *face conflicts on the job.*" "I am strong in the Lord; God's strength empowers me as I *face this difficult decision.*" "I am strong in the Lord; God's strength empowers me to *stand for justice.*"

Take time to relate this passage to internal or external conflicts that threaten your peace of mind or personal confidence.

I am strong in the Lord; God's strength empowers me as I
_____.

I am strong in the Lord; God's strength empowers me as I
_____.

I am strong in the Lord; God's strength empowers me to
_____.

I am strong in the Lord; God's strength empowers me to
_____.

EXERCISE TWO: LIVING BY YOUR IMAGINATION

In the quiet of your meditation, reflect on a conflict situation in your life. What is going on in this situation? What are your feelings about this conflict? How do you assess your own strengths in relationship to your challenges? As you imagine the conflict in all its complexity, you gradually discover that Christ is working deeply in your life and that your life is being supported by a power greater than yourself. As you imagine yourself rooted in Christ's infinite resourcefulness and strength, how do you feel? How does this change your perspective on this conflict situation? What new insights are you receiving that will enable you to resolve this conflict? Visualize the setting and your own empowered presence working to bring peace and justice to this personal or corporate conflict situation.

Close this time of meditative prayer by thanking God for the empowerment and insight that you have been given. Ask God to remind you that all the resources of the universe are yours when you stand for peace and justice. Commit yourself to seeking a creative resolution in this and every conflict situation.

Exercise Three: Faith in Action

The empowerment that Christ gives us is meant to be the catalyst for empowering others to become Christlike. Reflect on someone that you feel has been imprisoned by fear. Commit yourself to praying for his or her deliverance from fear. Pray that that person may experience Christ's infinite resourcefulness, protection, and power in his or her life. If the occasion presents itself and you have taken the time to listen to the person's deepest yearnings, with gentleness encourage her or him to explore God-given strengths.

A second option is to explore areas of conflict in your church or community. If you have a relationship with a conflict-ridden group, commit yourself to becoming a "nonanxious presence" and an instrument of peace. If you are in a position of leadership or consultation, explore nonviolent, collegial means of resolving differences, so that the various factions will grow in self-affirmation and affirmation of the others.

A decade after the crumbling of the Berlin Wall, our world is still at peril for nuclear war. Thousands of nuclear warheads still remain on a "hair-trigger alert," threatening holocaust in the blink of an eye. Congressional bodies refuse to seek the ways of peace and even vote against nuclear test ban treaties because they believe such treaties would threaten national security. Take time to educate yourself on the nuclear threat by seeking information from groups such as SANE or Physicians for Social Responsibility. Encourage your political leaders to seek a just peace and a safe world. You might also encourage them to seek to abolish landmines as well as nuclear weapons. In a world that believes that peace can only be assured by the threat of nuclear apocalypse, those who call themselves peacemakers must live by affirmations of life, trust, and alternative visions of our future.

My Faith in God Can Move Mountains

For truly I tell you, if you have faith the size of a mustard seed, you will say to this mountain, "Move from here to there," and it will move; and nothing will be impossible for you.

MATTHEW 17:20–21

Modern medicine is discovering that our attitudes can cure or kill us. Research has shown that the most hazardous time of the week is Monday morning. The negative attitudes people have toward their jobs may be a factor in workplace heart attacks. In contrast, it has been found that persons who have a deep trust in God are better able to cope with serious surgery, depression, and bereavement than those for whom religious faith is unimportant. Recently, a successful businesswoman shared with me her experiences with clinical depression. Although her depression led to suicidal thoughts and forced her to seek medical care, she asserted that only her hope in the future enabled her to go on in the darkest of days. Even today, her faith reminds her that she has a future in God's hands that cannot be destroyed by her intermittent periods of depression. In reflecting on his concentration camp experiences during the Holocaust, Victor Frankl asserted that those prisoners who had something to live for survived the indignities and hardships of the camps, while those who gave up hope soon succumbed to the diseases running rampantly through the camps.

Faith opens up to us new dimensions of reality and new sources of power. Faith is more than the assent to historic doctrines; it is the experience of the living reality of divine trustworthiness and adventure that gives substance to the historic doctrines of the church. When we open ourselves to the reality of divine faithfulness, the power of the universe—the energy that created the sun and brought our own lives into being—floods our minds and bodies, giving us new hope and new sight. From the perspective of faith, "Believing is seeing." Those who trust in God's abundance see the world in terms of abundant providence, unexpected insights, and life-changing possibilities. They see a path through the obstacles that can neither be avoided nor overcome.

One of my favorite healing stories involves the faith of friends that enabled a paralyzed man to find healing. As they carried the man to the house where Jesus was staying, they discovered that so many people had gathered around the house that there was no way they could take their friend in to see Jesus. At that moment, they were faced with a decision of life or death, of healing or illness. They could have gone home with the solace that they had done their best and that their friend would have to accept his brokenness of body and spirit. But they chose another path. As the crowd stared in astonishment, they climbed up the stairway at the edge of the house, laid their friend on the thatch roof, and began to tear the thatch and mud from the rooftop in order to let their friend down to see Jesus. They saw an opportunity amid the obstacles, a possibility amid the limitations.

Today's affirmation, at first glance, appears to place the possibility of growth and healing entirely in our hands. But look again at the scripture and at God's presence in your life. The faith of the friends was inspired by Jesus' healing power. Their image of the healing Christ led them up to the roof, calmed their fears of embarrassment, and empowered their hands to make a hole in the roof. Our faith is not in the experience of faith itself. Although our faith does activate the placebo effect, which energizes the body and enhances the immune system, our faith is more than just a placebo. It is lively confidence in the God incarnate in Jesus Christ. It is an open awareness to the divine possibilities that are already shaping our lives. In reality, as Luther and the Reformers proclaimed, our faith itself is a gift of God's grace. As important as our beliefs are in the formation of our lives, they have their ultimate origin in God's own process of spiritual formation, manifest in creative ideas, novel possibilities, and inspiring encounters.

While faith is not magic, it can contribute to our healing. When Mary came to see her pastor, she was desperate. She had just been diagnosed with cancer and, to her, cancer and death were synonymous. "I just want to go home and die," she confessed. "There's no hope for me now." After listening carefully to her hopelessness, her pastor asked Mary, "What is the prognosis of your cancer?" After a moment's silence, she confessed, "Well, the oncologist said that about half the people diagnosed with my kind of cancer will be alive in five years' time and may experience a complete remission, but half of them die before five years." Again, after a silent pause, her pastor asked, "Which half do you belong to? Are you one of the survivors, or will you be another victim?"

Although Mary could not predict her future, her pastor's question shocked her into seeing her life from a new perspective. With her pastor's support, she began to explore her attitudes toward cancer; but more important, she began to explore her attitudes about her own personal power and God's role in her life. Ultimately, Mary had a change of perspective. She discovered that she was not alone; she had friends, family, and Jesus to support her. She internalized her formerly abstract faith in divine providence and omnipresence. "God's providence and Christ's salvation are alive in my life. I feel God at work every moment of the day," she affirmed. She began to see God at work in chance encounters, in the biblical stories she read, in her growing optimism, and in the working of her immune system. As Mary began to use affirmations along with meditation, physical exercise, and chemotherapy, her mind was transformed. She even experienced greater physical energy and well-being than she had in years.

Today, Mary is one of the survivors. Although she does not claim that her newfound faith was the only cause of her healing, she asserts, "Without my trust in God's care and Christ's companionship, I know I would be dead today. When I began to trust God, I knew that I would be healed, even if the cancer was not cured. I knew that God was at work in my life and that whatever happened, God would be my companion." In changing her attitudes toward cancer, Mary changed her attitudes about life. Today, her "Expect a miracle" bumper sticker reflects her faith that whatever the future may bring, she will keep her eyes on Jesus. Mary's faith was born in the darkness and brought her into the light. As we claim the grace of Christ that awakens us to the power of the future, we can sing our affirmations of faith with countless Christians everywhere:

> My hope is built on nothing less than Jesus' blood and righteousness.
> I dare not trust the sweetest frame, but wholly lean on Jesus' name.
> On Christ the solid rock I stand, all other ground is sinking sand;
> all other ground is sinking sand.

> When darkness veils his lovely face, I rest on his unchanging grace.
> In every high and stormy gale, my anchor holds within the veil.
> On Christ the solid rock I stand, all other ground is sinking sand;
> all other ground is sinking sand.

> His oath, his covenant, his blood support me in the whelming flood.
> When all around my soul gives way, he then is all my hope and stay.
> On Christ the solid rock I stand, all other ground is sinking sand;
> all other ground is sinking sand.

> EDWARD MOTE, "MY HOPE IS BUILT"

What is the mountain in your way? What stands between you and the person God calls you to be? What keeps you from living out your "personal legend" and sharing God's love with the world? Empowerment comes step-by-step. Only faith the size of a mustard seed—a small alteration in your perception of reality and your vision of possibilities—can change your life forever, for God is working in your life, second by second, to provide the images of hope you need to take the next step and then the step that follows.

EXERCISE ONE: LIVING BY YOUR AFFIRMATIONS

At the heart of this affirmation is the trust that, amid the obstacles of life, our partnership with God will get us through. Simply take some time to affirm regularly, "My faith in God can move mountains."

In order to concretize this affirmation, relate it to your daily life or long-term personal issues. In my own life, I affirm: "My faith in God can move the mountain of *impatience in my life.*" "My faith in God can move the mountain of *fear of the future in my life.*" "My faith in God can move the mountain of *financial insecurity in my life.*"

In your own affirmations, reflect on the obstacles and mountains in your life in light of the interplay of God's grace and your faith.

My faith in God can move the mountain of _____.
My faith in God can move the mountain of _____.
My faith in God can move the mountain of _____.
My faith in God can move the mountain of _____.

EXERCISE TWO: LIVING BY YOUR IMAGINATION

After a few moments of relaxed quiet, visualize yourself on a journey to a beautiful land in which you expect to fulfill your dreams. What dreams are inspiring you today? What would it be like to live out your dreams?

As you see the promised land in the distance, you suddenly discover that your path is being blocked. What is blocking your path to the promised land? What obstacles stand in the way of embodying God's dream for you and your dream for yourself? Do you think you can overcome these obstacles in your path?

While you may experience some fear and anxiety as you confront these mountains in your way, you feel a presence working within your life, reminding you of the resources of God in addition to your own. You discover that Christ is standing beside you. What resources is God giving you to face these obstacles? Christ invites you to join him in clearing the obstacles that lie in the way. Visualize yourself and Christ picking up each obstacle and placing it at the side of the road. Beyond the obstacles you can see a glorious future and an exciting adventure ahead. With Christ as your companion, all the obstacles that lie ahead will be overcome.

As your steps lead you toward your dreams, take time to thank God for being the source of your faith and talent and your companion in the adventure of self-discovery.

EXERCISE THREE: FAITH IN ACTION

Many persons in our society believe that they are destined for poverty and failure as a result of the social and economic evils that stand in their way. Although these persons are not without resources, the obstacles grounded in social and economic injustice, neighborhood violence, and communal hopelessness may overcome the will of even the most talented of persons. Although personal growth requires facing the obstacles that life presents to us, certain obstacles are unnecessary and unjust, especially to the innocent spirit.

As you read the newspaper with eyes open to local, national, and global news, what social obstacles are currently destroying the lives of our children? In the quiet, consider what response to these obstacles God is calling forth in your life. We may choose to respond to the obstacle of homelessness by supporting Habitat for Humanity, or hunger by contributing to Save the Children, World Vision, Church World Service, or the Christian Children's Fund. You may encourage your church to organize a CROP Walk (for Church World Service) in your neighborhood. You may choose to become a mentor for an inner-city child or a coach for the local little league or soccer team (there are, after all, many latch-key children receiving little parental care, even in the upper-middle-class suburbs). As you look at the problem of disabled elders in our society, you may choose to volunteer for Meals on Wheels or choose a homebound elder in your church to adopt. Our faith comes alive when we experience our solidarity with persons in need and recognize that our fates are joined together.

God's Energy Constantly Flows through Me

*Abide in me as I abide in you. Just as the branch cannot
bear fruit by itself unless it abides in the vine, neither can
you unless you abide in me. I am the vine, you are the
branches. Those who abide in me and I in them bear
much fruit, because apart from me you can do nothing.*

JOHN 15:4–5

The new physics asserts that we live in an ocean of dynamically related energy. Within the holoverse, all things are joined experientially and energetically. We are a part of the whole, and the whole is present in each part. The Christian vision of reality also claims that we live within a sea of the Divine's energy, whose power is manifest in all things and whose love unites all things within the cosmic body of Christ.

Jesus of Nazareth was clearly an energy healer. Like an electrical transformer, his energy permeated each person he touched. In language reminiscent of today's energy medicine, the scriptures note that when the woman with the hemorrhage touched Jesus, a power flowed forth from him that made her whole. Jesus' healing energy transformed bodies, as well as spirits, as a sign of God's reign of shalom. In light of today's emerging global medicine, Jesus' healing touch opens the door for an appreciation of traditional Chinese medicine's understanding of universal, or *chi,* energy. Chinese acupuncture and acupressure, American therapeutic touch, and East-West *reiki,* I believe, manifest the same healing power as Jesus' healing touch and the traditional Christian practice of laying on of hands.

Today, many persons understand health and illness in terms of energy flow. When the universal energy is flowing in our lives, our minds and bodies are in sync. On the other hand, when the universal energy is blocked, we often experience the mental, emotional, and physical imbalances that may manifest in fatigue and disease. In the language of today's scripture, when we are alienated from this divine energy, we perish physically and spiritually: "Whoever does not abide in me is thrown away like a branch and withers" (v. 6).

The image of the vine and branches powerfully demonstrates our need to be in relationship with God. Alignment with God through

103

contemplative prayer, meditation, body prayer, and affirmation opens our whole being to a greater influx of divine healing energy. This energy, as medical researchers note, is revealed in the enhancement of the cardiovascular and immune systems and stress reduction, as well as in the peace of mind and experience of wholeness that is characteristic of spiritual growth. Yet the image of the vine and branches reminds us that health and wholeness involve connection with God and with our environments. Jesus' language points us to the power of the community committed to spiritual transformation. We bear fruit together as the energy of God flows through the whole and parts alike. A healthy vine involves all the branches and not just one part. As we align ourselves with God, the whole vine is nurtured, and as the other branches of the vine bear fruit, our own fruitfulness is enhanced.

Once again, bearing fruit is not primarily the result of our personal exertion. Rather, spiritual and physical well-being have their ground in God's graceful, life-enhancing, omnipresent energy. God is constantly nurturing us. We are bathed in divine power that gives us the power to bear much fruit. When we let this energy flow in and through us, we truly become a "new creation," a reflection of God's glory as human beings "fully alive." All we can do is give thanks to God for the energy that constantly creates and recreates.

> Creator God, creating still, by will and word and deed,
> create a new humanity to meet the present need.
>
> Redeemer God, redeeming still, with overflowing grace,
> pour out your love on us, through us, make this a holy place.
>
> Sustainer God, sustaining still, with strength for every day,
> empower us now to do your will. Correct us when we stray.
>
> Great Trinity, for this new day we need your presence still.
> Create, redeem, sustain us now to do your work and will.
>
> JANE PARKER HUBER, "CREATOR GOD, CREATING STILL"

EXERCISE ONE: LIVING BY YOUR AFFIRMATIONS

Take time to affirm, "God's energy constantly flows through me." Since fatigue is often the result of our state of mind, remember this affirmation when you are feeling physically drained. Become aware of God's infinite energy flowing through you as you affirm, "God's energy constantly flows through me." Experience the divine *ruach* (Hebrew for "breath" or "spirit") or the holy *pneuma* (Greek for "breath" or "spirit") flowing through you with every breath.

What would it mean to concretize this affirmation by relating it to your everyday life? In my own experience, I find myself energized as I breathe deeply while affirming: "God's energy is constantly flowing through me, *enabling me to accomplish everything I need to today.*" "God's energy is constantly flowing through me, *empowering me to complete the tasks ahead of me.*" "God's energy is constantly flowing through me, *giving me strength to bring healing to this situation.*"

Expand this affirmation to empower your own life. Experience an abundance of divine energy flowing through you to your neighbor, spouse, or friend, bringing vitality to each of your lives.

God's energy is constantly flowing through me, _____.
God's energy is constantly flowing through me, _____.
God's energy is constantly flowing through me, _____.
God's energy is constantly flowing through me, _____.

EXERCISE TWO: LIVING BY YOUR IMAGINATION

In the quiet, take time to breathe deeply, experiencing divine power flowing through your mind, body, and spirit. Visualize a lively, vital, growing grapevine. Image yourself as a green, growing branch on that vital vine. Experience God's energy flowing through you, constantly replenishing and enhancing your life, repairing any wounds or breaks. As the energy flows through you, your branch is becoming more and more fruitful. What fruit are you bearing today? What gifts are growing in your life?

Now, look at the wider perspective. Reflect on the vine as a whole. Experience the divine energy flowing through your life to your neighbors. Experience your own energy empowering the neighboring branches. What gifts does your branch give to the other branches?

EXERCISE THREE: FAITH IN ACTION

Listen to your whole person—body, mind, and spirit. How is the energy currently flowing in your life? Do you experience any areas where the divine energy is being blocked? Can you ascertain the source of these blocks? Take time to ask God's energy to flow through these blocks, making you whole and fruitful, and then visualize yourself in that "flow" state.

As you reflect on ways that you can open to the flow of divine energy, consider receiving and, possibly, learning a technique for enhancing the flow of healing energy: acupressure, acupuncture, massage, bioenergetics, reiki, or therapeutic touch.

Reflect on the importance of touch as a healing gift. Healing touch is always oriented toward the good of the receiver and, with the exception of infants and comatose persons, should be given only when the other desires it. As is appropriate and comfortable, experience God's healing energy flowing through you with every touch, whether it be a handshake, the passing of the peace, or an embrace. Commit yourself to using your hands only to heal and support other persons near you on the "vine" of life of which you are a part.

CHAPTER FOUR

The Spirit and the Forms of Love

Many mainstream and liberal Christians find the idea of the Holy Spirit virtually incomprehensible. As we look at the many widely publicized "pop" culture manifestations of the Holy Spirit, we often feel either repulsed or totally perplexed. Pentecostal and charismatic televangelists with their flashy testimonies, smug spiritual superiority, and dubious miracle stories both repel and fascinate us. Their ecstatic murmurings and exorbitant claims for healing and inspiration seem foreign to the rationalistic and orderly faith of mainstream and liberal Christians. But as we ponder their lively and ecstatic faith, we might ask ourselves if we are willing to let go of our need to control our spiritual lives and thought processes. I suspect that the wildly ecstatic and irrational practices evident among some charismatics offend and alienate us because, frankly, we are unconsciously envious of their deeply emotional faith in contrast to our typically "low-temperature" spirituality. We envy their growing churches, even though we find their exclusivist and conservative theologies repugnant in our pluralistic and scientific age. Looking over the spiritual fence, we wonder if there isn't some way that we can integrate vital, holistic spirituality and a lively sense of God's presence with a commitment to justice, inclusivity, and reason. In living by our denials, rather than by our affirmations, regarding the Holy Spirit, I believe that we often miss her presence in our midst. We should not forget that only three centuries ago the Quakers joined pacifism and a quest for justice with a deeply charismatic faith.

The Holy Spirit is profoundly iconoclastic. It blows where it wills, and often we can only see the rustling of the branches in its wake. When we try to put the Holy Spirit in a theological box or contol her manifestations, we find ourselves left spiritually empty-handed. Fiery and windy, yet intimately personal, the Spirit gives life to everything it touches. The tongues of fire and the rustling winds of Pentecost bring ecstasy in moments of private meditation as well as public worship. In its utter freedom, the Spirit is always the Spirit of Christ, always defined in terms of Christ's all-embracing, suffering, and healing love.

The presence of the Holy Spirit is known through the dynamic tension that draws us back and forth between life's polarities. The Spirit is intimate, but it drives us from solitude to community. The Spirit is unfettered, but it joins order and chaos in the quest for beauty of experience. The Spirit drives us, as persons and communities, toward novelty and innovation even as it preserves the gifts of tradition and established ritual. The Spirit disrupts and dislocates static forms of worship and polity while it cautions against rejecting the past. The Spirit inspires ecstatic self-transcendence as the unexpected companion of quiet spiritual centeredness. While it is universal in scope, the Spirit is intimate in its concreteness and particularity. Dramatic in its impact, the Spirit is also gentle in its influence. Who can control this divine breath that emerges in surprising and unexpected forms, and whose presence reveals *exactly* what is needed right where we are?

Ultimately, in all its forms and polar dynamics, the Holy Spirit is the manifestation of divine love and unity as it unites the fragmented soul and brings together diverse individuals into loving community. But even as it creates loving community, the Spirit of God drives us to expand the circle of love to include the "least of these" as well as the antagonists. Nothing is shut off from the Spirit, nor is anyone excluded from her loving, and often challenging, transformation.

In this third section of affirmations, we will embrace the two poles of the Spirit, represented by the inner journey of solitude and the outer journey of social transformation. In actuality, there is no opposition between these poles of solitude and community, even though we may emphasize one pole or the other in the spiritual lives of individuals or churches. For everything there is a season. In the harmonious, dynamic, and ecstatic movements of the Spirit, we are called to seek and find a creative, shifting balance that brings health to persons and communities.

In the Stillness, I Experience God

> God is our refuge and strength,
> a very present help in trouble.
> Therefore we will not fear, though the earth should
> change,
> though the mountains shake in the heart of the sea;
> though its waters roar and foam,
> though the mountains tremble with its tumult...
> "Be still, and know that I am God!
> I am exalted among the nations.
> I am exalted in the earth."
> The LORD of hosts is with us;
> the God of Jacob is our refuge.
>
> PSALM 46:1–3, 10–11

Many of us constantly seek to escape silence and solitude. We turn on the CD player or TV as soon as we get home. We listen to the news over the dinner table. Our eyes close listening to *Nightline,* David Letterman, or Jay Leno, and we awaken to the news on our radio alarm clock. As soon as we get in the car, we turn on the radio; even when we exercise, we carry our Walkman.

Noise pollution and a lack of solitude can be hazardous to your health. Larry Dossey notes that hurry sickness is a factor in many of today's illnesses. Even our recreation involves fast-paced activity. At an outdoor symphony concert this past summer, I saw one man checking e-mail on his laptop in the midst of Handel's *Water Music.* Even on a spiritual retreat, I have seen persons heading outdoors during break time, not for a brisk walk or a deep breath of country air but to check cellular phone messages. Like Martha from the gospel story, we are so busy multitasking that we forget what is most important in our lives—hospitality for our neighbor and for God.

Noise pollution in our national parks has become a matter of life and death for forest animals. Bombarded by the cacophony of stereos and CD players of people trying to get away from it all, the animals become so confused that they cannot hear the approach of their predators.

Our escape from silence is, no doubt, a symptom of our escape from the still, small voice of the Spirit speaking within our deepest selves. In our quest to fill our time with sound and activity, there is little room for God's spirit to speak to us, even in her "sighs too deep for words." A Buddhist story tells of a professor who sought an audience with a spiritually advanced monk. After introducing himself, he proceeded to launch into a philosophical discussion about the merits of the various forms of meditation. After a polite silence, the monk asked the professor if he would like a cup of tea. After the professor accepted his offer, the monk poured tea until the cup overflowed. As he continued to pour the tea, the surprised philosopher begged him to stop. The monk replied, "You are like this tea cup. You are filled with so many words that there is no room for me to teach you anything. You must empty yourself to experience the truth."

Psalm 46 asserts that even in the maelstrom of external conflict we can find a quiet place. Yet in today's world, the experience of peace must be a matter of intentionality and discipline. Abraham Joshua Heschel reminds us that the world was created for the Sabbath. Action exists so that there may be rest. Words exist so that there may be meaningful silence. But we can only experience sabbath time when we turn off the TV or CD player, put away the computer or cell phone, and invite the deep silence of God to speak within us. Even within the earth-shaking conflicts of life, the psalmist affirms, we can find a minisabbath, a stillpoint amid the shifting world. In silence, we discover that the God of Jacob is our refuge. "Be still and know that I am God." In the words of a contemporary hymn, God calls us to come and find the quiet center:

> Come and find the quiet center in the crowded life we lead,
> find the room for hope to enter, find the frame where we are freed:
> clear the chaos and the clutter, clear our eyes, that we can see
> all the things that really matter, be at peace, and simply be.
>
> Silence is a friend who claims us, cools the heat and slows the pace,
> God it is who speaks and names us, knows our being, touches base,
> making space within our thinking, lifting shades to show the sun,
> raising courage when we're shrinking, finding scope for faith begun.
>
> In the Spirit let us travel, open to each other's pain,
> let our loves and fears unravel, celebrate the space we gain:
> there's a place for deepest dreaming, there's a time for heart to care,
> in the Spirit's lively scheming there is always room to spare!

SHIRLEY ERENA MURRAY, "COME AND FIND THE QUIET CENTER"

It is important to remember that the Spirit speaks in all things. All creatures are icons of God. All events reveal God's wisdom to us. But we must be still to listen for the still, small voice of the Holy Spirit moving through all things. In the spacious silence born of our commitment to contemplative prayer, we find rest and perspective even on the busiest of days. Like Brother Lawrence, we can discover that the spirit of God is as present in the mundane tasks of the kitchen as it is at the communion table.

It has been said that you can always find the caregiver and social activist: He or she is the one always rushing around with the frown and furrowed brow! While it is well known that burnout is the occupational hazard of anyone who seeks to embody God's aim at justice and love in the interpersonal and corporate spheres of life, we must remember that burnout is a choice. When we neglect the discipline of silence, we soon find ourselves without resources to face the noisy crowd. The Spirit moves freely between silence and action, solitude and community, and invites us to find balance and health through contemplative action and active contemplation.

Exercise One: Living by Your Affirmations

As you embody this affirmation, take time to repeat, "In stillness, I experience God." An alternative affirmation might be "God is my refuge and strength."

Concretizing this affirmation in my own life, I have personalized it in the following fashion: "In stillness, I experience God's presence in *this conflict*." "God is my refuge and strength as I *work for justice in this situation*." "In stillness, I experience God's presence in *this interview*." "God is my refuge and strength in *my financial life*."

In what areas of your life do you need to concretize this affirmation? As you look at the week ahead, what challenges are you facing? Perhaps you might focus on God's presence in these upcoming situations. The point is not to deny conflict, but to discover God's presence as your strength and shield in the midst of conflict and challenge.

In stillness, I experience God's presence in _____.
In stillness, I experience God's presence as I _____.
God is my refuge and strength in _____.
God is my refuge and strength as I _____.

Exercise Two: Living by Your Imagination

In this section, I would invite you to explore the experience of silence through a variety of meditative practices.

112 *The Power of Affirmative Faith*

Centering Prayer. This form of meditative prayer has been revived for the modern age by Roman Catholic spiritual guides Thomas Keating and Basil Pennington. The technique is simple and straightforward. At the heart of centering prayer is one's focus on a meaningful prayer word (for example: light, God, Christ, peace, shalom) as a means of discovering the divine silence within all things. The process consists of the following steps:

(1) Find a comfortable and quiet place.

(2) Close your eyes.

(3) Say a brief prayer for openness to God.

(4) Begin to repeat your prayer word or focus word.

(5) When your mind wanders or you are distracted, simply return to the prayer word without judgment or self-condemnation.

(6) Close your prayer time with the Lord's Prayer or any meaningful blessing.

(7) Gently return to your daily tasks.

Ideally, one practices centering prayer twice each day for fifteen to twenty minutes. Centering prayer brings a sense of calm to body, mind, and spirit.

Breath Prayer. The Holy Spirit is often described in terms of breath or *pneuma*. As the one "in whom we live, move, and have our being," God inspires us with each breath. Breath prayer is an especially important spiritual discipline, because many persons experience an inability to breathe deeply during times of stress and spiritual decenteredness. Breathing with the Holy Spirit enables us to experience God's energizing and centering breath in even the most challenging moments of our lives.

In breath prayer, you can simply observe your breath with a sense of mindfulness, noting your wandering thoughts and bringing them back to the breath of God moving through you.

You may also choose to say a brief word with each breath. My own teacher, Alan Armstrong Hunter, taught breath prayer in the following manner: As you inhale, simply say, "I breathe the Spirit deeply in"; as you exhale, "I breathe the Spirit out again." You may also use the exhaling to identify and let go of feelings; for example, "I breathe the Spirit deeply in, I breathe it anxiously out again." As you exhale, commit those feelings to God's care.

Quaker silence. In the spirit of the Quakers, for whom structured liturgies are often seen as an impediment to God's presence, take time just to be still with the intent to experience and receive guidance from the inner light of Christ within you. Listen for the voice of God, whose depth is silence, welling up from within the many voices.

EXERCISE THREE: FAITH IN ACTION

Intentionally make a commitment to "be still" in God's presence in situations that often try your patience. For example, recently I discovered that my medical insurance company had failed to reenroll me in a new plan following my departure from Georgetown University. To say the least, I was angry. But as I waited to speak with the representative, I took time to "be still" by breathing deeply and centering myself in God so that while I would be clear in my grievance, I would not take my anger out on the powerless customer service representative. When I finally had an opportunity to speak with her, my words were direct, clear, and assertive, but they were also friendly and cooperative.

Use inconveniences as opportunities to cultivate the experience of God's peace in your life. Check-out counters at the supermarket provide a wonderful opportunity for spiritual discipline. Rather than becoming angry or anxious, take time to notice your breathing. As you breathe the Spirit in, blow it out as a blessing on the check-out attendant or on the people in line in front of you.

Sabbath time. Spiritual guide Tilden Edwards has written about the importance of sabbath time for mental and spiritual well-being. In that spirit, I have recently chosen to take Sundays off for re-creation through family time, meditation, and spiritual and recreational reading. Although it is occasionally difficult not to study or make business calls on Sundays, I have found that this day of rest blesses the rest of the week. If you cannot take a whole day, commit a few minutes every day for quiet time, a few hours once a week for creative solitude, and a few days each year for a spiritual growth retreat.

The Spirit Speaks to Me in Sighs
Too Deep for Words

*Likewise the Spirit helps us in our weakness; for we do
not know how to pray as we ought, but that very Spirit
intercedes with sighs too deep for words.*

ROMANS 8:26

The Franciscan theologian Saint Bonaventure asserts that "every
creature is a word of God because it speaks of God." Bonaventure's
affirmation, along with Romans 8:26, has been one of the guiding
principles of this book's understanding of theology and spiritual formation.
God's spirit is with us from the inside as well as the outside. We are
constantly the objects of divine affection and inspiration. God, who "in
all things is working for good," is at work in the deepest interstices of
our lives.

Our deepest identity is the reality of God's intimate and personal
voice, calling us within our own unique gifts for self-discovery and service.
Whether or not we are aware of it, we are always receiving the guidance
and care that we need. God's wisdom is always being revealed within
the still, small voice that speaks in "sighs too deep for words."

Sadly, most of time we feel bereft of wisdom and insight. We go
from crisis to crisis, failing to see God's guiding light in the midst of
chaos and confusion. Amid all the voices that would direct us, there is
one holy voice that knows what is best for us always and everywhere.

We attune ourselves to that voice by using the gentle practices of
silent contemplation and focused meditation, and by simply asking, "God,
show me the way; give me your wisdom and light. Let me hear your
voice within all the other voices." In the language of the apostle Paul,
when we open to the voice of the Spirit, we are no longer conforming to
the world, but are transforming our lives by the renewal of our minds.

One of my favorite biblical stories is God's calling of the young boy
Samuel during a time of national dislocation. In the quiet of the night,
Samuel hears a voice; "Samuel, Samuel," it whispers. Thinking it is Eli
the high priest, Samuel rushes to his mentor's side. But it is not Eli who
calls. Again, in the night, Samuel hears the voice, "Samuel, Samuel."

114

Twice again, Samuel hears his name called. Each time, he seeks out the sleeping Eli, who finally intuits that the nocturnal voice may be the voice of God. When he hears the voice once more, Samuel replies, "Speak, for your servant listens." We do not hear because we do not listen. Tranquilized by the trivial and confused by competing voices, we often let the quiet voice of God go unnoticed. But when we follow Samuel's example and simply say, "Here I am; speak, for I am listening," our whole world becomes an epiphany and each moment a revealing of divine insight. In the refrain of a popular campus hymn:

> Here I am, Lord. Is it I, Lord? I have heard you calling in the night.
> I will go, Lord, if you lead me. I will hold your people in my heart.
>
> DANIEL L. SCHUTTE, "HERE I AM, LORD"

Within Romans 8 we find a relational model for spiritual formation. First, spiritual growth begins with the humble spirit of agnosticism. As Paul asserts, "We do not know how to pray as we ought." In this great "I don't know," we open ourselves to hearing the voice of the Spirit, unfiltered by our own preconceptions and doctrinal certainties. Often we think we know God so well that we end up not recognizing God's guiding presence when it is right before us. Humility invites us to simply listen for the voice that speaks beneath and within all the other voices.

Second, spiritual formation is grounded in the recognition of our relatedness to all of creation. Paul asserts that creation—in all its forms—is groaning in light of God's aim for it. As we listen deeply for the Spirit, we hear the voice of God speaking through the poor and lonely, the suffering and dying, the human and nonhuman. Our deepest needs—our personal petitions and intercessions for others—are always contextual. Our greatest good is always found in light of the good of all things. The God who speaks through sparrows and donkeys can call us to transformation in any setting and by any media.

Third, we are challenged to be mindful, that is, to listen closely to our inner thoughts and motivations in order to discern which voices truly reflect our deepest spiritual needs and which have arisen merely from the voices of our parents and our cultures. In relationships and in spiritual formation, we have to make a conscious effort to let go of our projections and conditioning in order to experience the spacious presence of God where we are in this moment. Life is always adventurous when we remember that God's voice is speaking to us every second of the day. When we let go of our need to control the Divine by our own politics, religions, or perspectives, God's holy adventure constantly surprises and energizes us.

EXERCISE ONE: LIVING BY YOUR AFFIRMATIONS

Today, we simply set aside time to repeat, "The Spirit speaks to me in sighs too deep for words," and then to listen in the quiet. We can personalize this affirmation in many ways: "The Spirit is speaking to me in this situation" or "I experience God's guidance in every situation."

In my own life, I have concretized this affirmation by remembering: "The Spirit speaks to me in *this moment of meditation.*" "The Spirit speaks to me as I *listen to my son's voice.*" "The Spirit speaks to me as I *talk with my wife.*" "The Spirit speaks to me *and will provide an answer to this problem.*" A friend who suffers from an anxiety disorder that occasionally hinders her deep breathing says to herself, "The Spirit speaks to me when I *sigh deeply.*"

Take time to look at your own life. Where do you need God's guidance today? Where do you need to hear the divine voice amid all the other voices of life?

The Spirit speaks to me as I _____.

The Spirit speaks to me as I _____.

The Spirit speaks to me when I _____.

The Spirit speaks to me in _____.

EXERCISE TWO: LIVING BY YOUR IMAGINATION

In this section, we will embody the affirmation through two meditative exercises.

In the first, the goal is silent listening. Although each of us hears the Spirit's sighs in a unique fashion, the following variation of "centering prayer" may be helpful to you:

(1) Find a comfortable position.

(2) Relax a few moments, noting any places of stress or fatigue and letting go of them.

(3) Speak a prayer for guidance and for the ability to listen.

(4) Listen in the silence, hearing the many voices, opening to the deepest voice of the Spirit.

(5) Close with a prayer of thanksgiving, acknowledging the conscious or unconscious wisdom you have received.

In this and many of the other exercises in this book, you may choose to spend a few moments journaling on your insights or any questions that may have emerged. The spiritual discipline of journaling helps us to be attentive to the intersection of God's voice and our own voices.

A Visualization on the Call of Samuel. In this visualization, begin with a moment of silent relaxation. Let your mind wander in the stillness of the night. As you lie in bed, explore your environment. Where are you? What is your room like? In the quiet, you hear a voice calling your name. What does it sound like? In your visualization, after you hear the voice, go to your companion and ask if he or she is calling.

You return to your bed. But you hear the voice calling you again and again by name. Still, you do not recognize it. When you hear it one more time, you intuit that this may be the voice of God. You respond by saying, "Speak; your servant is listening."

What does this voice have to say to you? What insight is it giving you? What counsel can you integrate into your daily life?

Close this time of reflection with a prayer of gratitude for God's inspiration and a petition that God will enable you to be attentive to the Spirit throughout your day. (One of the gifts of this exercise is that it can be used whenever you are uncertain of a decision that lies ahead of you. Even if you do not receive a clear answer or inspiration, it reminds you to attend to the voice of God and may awaken you to synchronous insights and encounters that you would otherwise miss.)

EXERCISE THREE: FAITH IN ACTION

Methodist spiritual guide Maxie Dunnam invites persons to use the following affirmation: "I give Christ to and receive Christ from everyone I meet." Take time to remember this affirmation as you awaken in the morning, as you interact with family or friends, as you dialogue in the workplace, or as you meet a stranger. In living with this affirmation, we attune ourselves to the Spirit's voice speaking to us in the voices of others and within our own voices. It reminds us that as we give and receive Christ in our relationships with others, we may be answers to their prayers or solutions to their problems, as they may be to ours.

This affirmation also reminds us of the importance of listening to one another. True listening requires tremendous mindfulness. We need to let go of finishing other people's sentences or thinking of our replies before they have finished speaking. With our families, we need to be still before we respond, especially in situations of conflict and disagreement. Before you speak, listen for God and ask for God's guidance in your reply.

In your next conversation, simply listen with the heart as well as the mind. What is the deep word your partner is seeking to communicate? What gift of love can you give to her or him?

As we seek to be attentive to the Holy Spirit, we overcome the dualism of mind and body, spirit and flesh, and individual and community that plagues much of Western and Eastern spirituality. In the deeply woven fabric of life that is affirmed by process-relational spirituality, contemplation, action, and embodiment are intimately connected with one another.

God Speaks to Me in Dreams

I will pour out my Spirit upon all flesh,
and your sons and your daughters shall prophesy, and
your young men shall see visions,
and your old men shall dream dreams.
Even upon my slaves, both men and women,
in those days I will pour out my Spirit;
and they shall prophesy.

ACTS 2:17–18

In the human experience, consciousness is just the tip of the iceberg, beneath which lie myriad unconscious images, memories, and influences. Nevertheless, certain types of traditional Christianity have been uneasy with the unconscious. In contrast to the clear, distinct, and controllable world of theological doctrines and congregational governance, the unconscious—like the Spirit itself—is untamed and goes where it wills. Repressed or left alone, the unconscious may destructively intrude on conscious behaviors through "Freudian slips," inappropriate relational patterns, and deep-seated fears and anxieties. It is my belief that God is present in every aspect of our experience, including such manifestations of the unconscious. Accordingly, it is necessary that spiritual transformation embrace and heal the unconscious as well as the conscious mind.

In ancient times, dreams were seen as vehicles of divine communication. These nocturnal visitors from the unconscious revealed important truths that the everyday consciousness could not access on its own. Although these dreams may have been frightening, they often provided valuable spiritual and political guidance. Long before the innovative dream work of the Swiss psychiatrist Carl Jung, the biblical tradition bore witness to the divine presence in both unconscious and superconscious experiences. In beginning the day at sunset rather than dawn, the Hebraic people recognized that God is at work in our sleeping as well as waking lives. Joseph's ability to interpret his own and others' dreams enabled him to become a trusted advisor to Pharaoh. Joseph, the father of Jesus, considered separating from Mary until the angel of the Lord appeared to him in a dream, saying, "Joseph, son of David, do

119

not fear to take Mary for your wife, for that which is conceived in her is of the Holy Spirit." Later, Joseph was warned in a dream to escape from the wrath of Herod by taking his family to Egypt. After Herod's death, the angel of the Lord once more appeared, inviting Joseph to take Mary and Jesus back to Israel. The magi who followed the star in search of the Messiah were also warned in a dream to return to their own lands without reporting to King Herod.

The spread of the early church was facilitated through Peter's visionary dream of the clean and unclean foods. When Peter protested against God's invitation to eat the unclean foods, God commanded Peter to call nothing unclean. Just moments later, messengers arrived from the Gentile Cornelius, bidding Peter to come to his household and baptize his family and servants.

Clearly, God *speaks* to humankind through visions and dreams. Our sighs too deep for words initially emerge from the unconscious, and only by our attention and openness can these deep stirrings become available to shape our conscious experiences. Although our dreams and divine insights shape us even when we are not aware of them, their power and guidance is magnified when we invite them into our conscious experiences. In the spirit of Celtic spirituality, we can call on God to be our guide by night and by day:

> Be thou my vision, O Lord of my heart;
> naught be all else to me, save that thou art
> thou my best thought by day or by night,
> waking or sleeping, thy presence my light.

> EIGHTH-CENTURY IRISH SONG, TRANSLATED BY MARY BYRNE,
> VERSED BY ELEANOR HULL, "BE THOU MY VISION"

Still, we must remember that the unconscious—like every other aspect of human experience—is ambiguous. It contains light and shadow, health and disease, good and evil, divine and demonic. Although healthy spiritual integration is built upon embracing the shadow side as well as the light, we must ask for the spirit of discernment to enable us to tell the difference between healing and harmful dreams. If we are perplexed by the dreams we experience, we would do well to consult with a spiritual guide or pastoral counselor who is skilled in dream interpretation, even as we ask God to enable us to understand and appropriately live out the wisdom of our dreams. Nevertheless, the inspiration of dreams and visions constantly challenges us to expand our understanding of revelation. Not encompassed by the pages of any book, even the Bible, the Spirit addresses us through deep sighs, mystical visions, intuitive hunches, synchronous events, insightful books, and surprising encounters. These events testify to God's desire that each person encounter God's grace and inspiration in a personal and intimate way.

EXERCISE ONE: LIVING BY YOUR AFFIRMATIONS

In times of perplexity and conflict, many people ask God for a healing dream, that is, a dream that will help bring about wholeness in a particular situation in their lives. In my life, I found that I did not remember my dreams until I took a course on myth and dream interpretation in college. In taking the course, I opened the door to a whole new realm of insight and inspiration. Others find their dream lives becoming more vivid when they begin to journal about their dreams or begin counseling with a therapist skilled in dream interpretation.

If you feel called to experience God's presence in your dreams, take time to affirm, "God is speaking to me through my dreams, and I am listening for God's guidance." To concretize this affirmation, I have personalized it in the following manner: "God is speaking to me in dreams related to *my vocational future.*" "God is speaking me in dreams related to *my conflict with* _____." "God is speaking to me in dreams related to *the book I am writing.*"

Take a moment to ponder God's place in your unconscious as well as conscious life. What questions need answers in your spiritual life? What life concerns need *questions* asked about them? Where do you need God's guidance or inspiration?

God is speaking to me in dreams related to _____.
God is speaking to me in dreams related to _____.
God is speaking to me in dreams related to _____.
God is speaking to me in dreams related to _____.

EXERCISE TWO: LIVING BY YOUR IMAGINATION

One way to open to God's wisdom in your dreams is to take a few minutes each night before retiring simply to be still and ask God if there is anything that your unconscious needs to reveal to you. You may invoke a particular situation or ask God for a healing dream. Close your prayer, in the spirit of the traditional evening devotion of Compline, by asking for divine protection in the night.

As you awaken in the morning, take time before you plunge into the day's activities to reflect on the night that has passed. Do you remember any dreams? What were they like? Did they feel comfortable or frightening? Do you hear the voice of God in the dream?

Some people like to take a few extra moments to relax, close their eyes, and then through visualization complete what may have been uncertain or incomplete in the dream. In this "waking dream," the answers you are looking for may emerge.

Following the guidance of Ira Progoff's work on dream journaling, many persons, such as my wife, Kate, keep a dream journal. The purpose of this journal is to enable you to remember your dreams, explore their meaning in your life over a long period of time, and discover connections in your dream life. Such journals enable people to experience the variety of ways that God is speaking to them through their dreams.

EXERCISE THREE: FAITH IN ACTION

You may find greater insight into your dreams if you participate in a dream interpretation group. Often, the local Jung Society can provide information about dream groups or therapists who specialize in dream interpretation. If you are in a covenant prayer group, you might suggest that the group consider reflecting on the many ways that God communicates to humankind (prayers, visions, hunches, dreams, synchronous encounters).

In light of what you have learned about the diversity of divine revelation, listen carefully and without judgment to other persons' reports of nonrational experiences. Rather than immediately dismissing them as irrelevant or strange, take time to explore the wisdom in their experiences. It has been said that the mystic and the lunatic are found in the same waters, but the mystic knows how to swim. As you explore your own inner spiritual landscape and dialogue with other spiritual adventurers, what can you learn from a critical and prayerful openness to the insight of dreams, visions, and near-death experiences that have become commonplace in recent years?

My Body Is the Temple of God

> *Do you not know that your body is a temple of the Holy*
> *Spirit within you, which you have from God, and that you*
> *are not your own? For you were bought with a price;*
> *therefore glorify God in your body.*
>
> 1 CORINTHIANS 6:19–20

Your body is a temple of God. How odd that statement seems to many Christians today. Although the Gnostic belief in the evil of embodiment was defined as heresy by the early church, many Christians are still Gnostic in their outlook. To them, faith primarily relates to the fate of the disembodied soul. Our bodies are seen as lust-full impediments to our ultimate spiritual vocations. The bodies of women, most especially, have been seen as "occasions for sin" to those men who sought to be pure before God.

Although monastic attitudes toward the body no longer prevail, many Christians are still ambivalent toward their bodies. On the one hand, there is a somatic hedonism that infects our culture and its attitudes toward sexuality, diet, and affluence. In quest of sensual pleasure, many persons go from one partner or one drug to another in search of "technical ecstasy," forgetting that authentic sensuality involves the whole person and not just physical technique and gratification. On the other hand, others seek to satisfy the "lusts of the flesh" through gastrointestinal hedonism or unbridled opulence. Tragically, others mortify the flesh through anorexia and other eating disorders. As we enter one diet program after another, we forget the other "weight problem," the malnutrition that destroys both the bodies and minds of thousands of children in the developing world and impoverished parts of the United States.

Today, more than ever, we need a spirituality of embodiment that challenges us to cherish the well-being of our own bodies as well as the bodies of other persons. Christian spirituality is ultimately a creation spirituality. The heavens declare the glory of God; the grasses and birds reveal God's providential care. Closer to home, our skin joins us in love with our spouse, children, or the comfort of friends. Our kidneys, intestines, and cardiovascular system reveal God's care for the basics of existence. When God looks at embodiment—and our particular embodiment—God proclaims it to be "good." Still, despite God's affirmation of embodiment, many of us have poor bodily images that reflect and condition our physical health. We are dissatisfied with the sizes of our stomachs and our sexual organs. We compare ourselves with magazine supermodels and male movie stars. We are seduced by the "world's" image of beauty, which blinds us to the authentic beauty of our own bodies and the bodies of our neighbors, be they young or old. God speaks words of joy and words of warning through our bodies to those attentive enough to hear.

"Your body is a temple of the Holy Spirit, a temple of God." In that passage, we discover that the body is a holy place, a sanctuary where God is present and revealed. Our bodies were made by God's love and are permeated through and through by mind and spirit. Biblical theology is ultimately holistic in its understanding of the unity of the body, mind, spirit, and relationship. Our bodies are gifts of God that demand affirmation and care. Surely this is what the apostle Paul means when he proclaims, "Glorify God in your body." While glorifying God through embodiment includes, as Paul notes, appropriate sexual morality and fidelity, it also includes a commitment to self-care in terms of what we eat and drink as well as proper rest and exercise.

In caring for our bodies, we discover that ours is profoundly related to the body of Christ. The Spirit that moves in our embodiment flows through the Christian community and wider planetary community. In the meeting ground of our bodies and the body of Christ, personal and social morality are joined, for we cannot be fully healthy ourselves while children starve, violence undermines love, and sexuality is exploited. We are called to "live simply so that others may simply live," and we are called to speak for God's family values of respect, affirmation, and hospitality. We love God best when we love creation in all its variety as the image of God. Our affirmation of the divine embodiment that calls us to enjoyment and justice is reflected in the words of Thomas Troeger:

Holy and good is the gift of desire.
God made our bodies for passion and fire,
intending that love would draw from the flame
lives that would shine with God's image and name.

God weeps for people abandoned, abused.
God weeps for people whose bodies are bruised.
God weeps when the flame that God has infused
is turned from its purpose and brutally used.

God calls to women and God calls to men:
"Don't hide from terror, or terror will win.
I made you for love, but love must begin
by facing the violence without and within."

THOMAS H. TROEGER, "HOLY AND GOOD IS THE GIFT OF DESIRE"

God's spirit of shalom—the spirit of the divinely animated temple—invites all of us to glorify good in the taste of good food, with the touch of a hand, through a longing embrace, in dance, and in sport. Love God in the world of the flesh—and proclaim the glory of God in everyone's flesh, everyone's health, everyone's joy.

EXERCISE ONE: LIVING BY YOUR AFFIRMATIONS

As we seek to transform our images of embodiment, let us live by the countercultural affirmation: "My body is the temple of God." I have concretized this in my life by expanding the affirmation: "My body is the temple of God; *I treat it with respect and care*." "My body is the temple of God; *I exercise regularly and eat wisely*." "My body is the temple of God; *I respect the bodies of others*."

In what ways would you personalize this affirmation? Take a moment to relate it to your own personal experience of embodiment.

My body is the temple of God; _____.
My body is the temple of God; _____.
My body is the temple of God; _____.
My body is the temple of God; _____.

EXERCISE TWO: LIVING BY YOUR IMAGINATION

Take time to relax, breathing deeply God's peaceful and healing presence. You may wish to lie down for this visualization. After a few minutes, visualize God's healing light entering your body with each breath. Experience it filling your body with healing light, beginning with your lungs…passing through your cardiovascular system…your head…neck…shoulders…immune system…chest…stomach and solar plexus…digestive system…sexual and reproductive organs…hips…thighs…legs…feet…Feel God's healing touch permeating your whole being, bringing vitality of mind and body.

Do you notice any tense parts of your body? Surround these with a healing light.

Do you notice any areas of "shame" or "embarrassment"? Surround these with a healing light as you remind yourself that these parts are essential to the temple.

Do you notice any weak or diseased parts of your body? Surround these with a healing light, and visualize this divine light energizing and strengthening your whole being as well as the particular part.

Are you struggling with any addictions or excesses? Surround these with a healing light, and ask for God's deliverance.

Close this time of visualization with a prayer of thanksgiving for God's gift of embodiment.

EXERCISE THREE: FAITH IN ACTION

In embodying this affirmation, commit yourself to nurturing the temple of God with which you have been entrusted. You may consider a commitment to the following:

(1) an appropriate exercise program, after consulting with your healthcare giver (some possibilities include swimming, walking, gentle jogging, yoga, T'ai Chi);

(2) regular time for quiet and meditation;

(3) body prayer and dance;

(4) an appropriate diet, for both good health and the well-being of others;

(5) walking prayer (that is, integrating your affirmations or prayer work with your daily exercise routine).

Focusing on the body as the temple of God also challenges us to care for the temples of our brothers and sisters. This is especially important, because one of the primary determinants of a person's health over his or her whole lifetime is the economic welfare and educational level of his or her parents. In the developing nations, malnutrition is a major cause of mental retardation. Within the body of Christ, every body is important and must be cherished.

In this spirit, "loving God in the world of the flesh" calls us to action. Consider one or more of the following:

(1) Join a hunger awareness group such as Bread for the World and follow national policies regarding hunger, health care, and education.

(2) Look at the health care resources in your city or nation. In what ways can you support more inclusive health care programs?

(3) Propose that your church begin a health care ministry. This can involve high-pressure screening and other health

enhancement programs as well as classes in meditation and stress reduction.

(4)   Look at your own eating habits in terms of global malnutrition. How can you cook nutritious and good-tasting meals in light of a "diet for a small planet"?

(5)   Volunteer at a soup kitchen, taking the time to get to know the homeless who come to eat there.

An Aerobic Walking Meditation. For a number of years, I have sought to embody the essential unity of spirit, mind, body, vocation, and relationship in my early-morning walking meditation. Although this approach does not require a set time or speed, I believe that its practice can bring wholeness to every aspect of our lives. As I describe my daily practice, I invite you to adapt it to your own needs and philosophy of life. In my case, I feel comfortable joining biblical affirmations with the emphasis on energy characteristic of Chinese philosophy and medicine. I focus on the seven centers of my body, breathing in and out the spirit of God as I repeat specific affirmations related to each of these energy centers. I will briefly describe a process that takes between fifteen and thirty minutes. If your mind should wander during this walking meditation, bring it back to your focus without judgment.

Top of the head: As I breathe in and out three times, I affirm "divine wisdom."

Forehead: As I breathe in and out three times, I affirm "divine intelligence and order."

Throat: As I breathe in and out three times, I affirm "God's healing words."

Heart: As I breathe in and out three times, I affirm "divine love and courage."

Solar plexus: As I breathe in and out three times, I affirm "divine health and vitality."

Genitals: As I breathe in and out three times, I affirm "divine creativity and sexuality."

Anus: As I breathe in and out three times, I affirm "divine forgiveness and letting go."

Once I have completed my breathing and affirmations, moving downward from the top of the head to the anus, I repeat the process, moving upward from the anus to the top of the head, envisaging God's energy permeating my being with each breath and adding a particular affirmation or affirmations to each of the seven centers. Here are the specific affirmations that I add as I breathe in and out divine energy, following my initial affirmations listed above.

Anus: "I let go and let God." "I let go of the past and open to God's future."

Genitals: "I respond creatively to every life situation." "I am growing in intimacy and love with my wife."

Solar plexus: "I can do all things through Christ who strengthens me; I am a powerhouse." (At this center, I lift up my petitions for projects and material well-being.)

Heart: "I am strong in the Lord." "Nothing can separate me from the love of God." "My heart beats with health and vitality and love and courage." (At this center, I lift up my prayers for others as I hold them in my heart.)

Throat: "Let the words of my mouth and the meditations of my heart be acceptable in thy sight, O God, my rock and my salvation."

Forehead: "My God shall supply all my needs." "I align myself with divine intelligence and order." (At this center, I lift up specific needs with the affirmation "My God shall supply my need for _____.")

Top of the head: "God's wisdom constantly flows through me, providing me with guidance and insight."

I Am Part of the Body of Christ

For just as the body is one and has many members, and
all the members of the body, though many, are one body,
so it is with Christ. For in the one Spirit we were all
baptized into one body—Jews or Greeks, slaves or free—
and we were all made to drink of one Spirit…If one
member suffers, all suffer together with it; if one member
is honored, all rejoice together with it.

1 CORINTHIANS 12:12–13, 26

The spirit of God invites us to journey from solitude to community. In the words of Genesis, human beings are not meant to be alone. The Spirit that brings integrity and vitality in moments of quiet reflection to the individual is also the source of the integrity and vitality of the communities within which our lives are nurtured. In a world of diversity, the Spirit brings a unity in which the gift of each person, tradition, gender, and faith is affirmed. Indeed, the divine Spirit is the source of creative diversity. In Paul's image of the body of Christ, the body could not function with just a head, feet, stomach, or ears (1 Cor. 12:12–27). The hidden parts of the body—the digestive, reproductive, immune, and cardio-vascular systems—are more essential to the well-being of the body than the more obvious and noticable parts. Yet each part requires the others for its well-being. Each part, by fulfilling its function, contributes to the well-being of the whole.

Within the body of Christ, diversity is a call for celebration and affirmation. As we relate to the diversity of gifts, colors, personality types, religious traditions, genders, and sexual orientations, our calling is to bring forth the gifts of our neighbor without defensiveness, envy, or superiority.

Within the body of Christ, self-affirmation drives us to mutual affirmation and loving support. The divine circle that centers on my life also centers on my neighbor's life. Relationality and individuality are balanced by the creative and dynamic interdependence of the Spirit that joins all things. As the mind of the body, the Spirit of Christ is immanent in all of the parts in the same way that our mind permeates the totality of our organism.

Within the body of Christ, we all need one another in order to achieve our fullest self-actualization. As the apostle Paul asserts, the diverse members of the body are called to have care for one another: "If one member suffers, all suffer together; if one member is honored, all rejoice together." On the macrocosmic level, the body of Christ reflects what we discover on the microcosmic level of psychosomatic unity. Nineteen hundred years after Paul's affirmation, Martin Luther King, Jr., spoke of the body of Christ in terms of the "beloved community" that embraced all of humanity, despite its diversity. According to King, all persons "are caught in an inescapable network of mutuality, tied in a single garment of destiny. Whatever affects one directly affects all indirectly. I can never be what I ought to be until you are what you ought to be, and you can never be what you ought to be until I am what I ought to be."[1]

Love is the force that brings life to the body. If God is love, then the Spirit is the embodiment of this love within the many relationships of our lives. The Spirit's love joins us with one another and inspires us to widen the circle of love to include the whole planet. Within the body, even confrontation must be motivated and manifested in love. On the microcosmic level of the human body, many persons responding to cancer or AIDS have chosen not to hate the disease, but to embrace and surround it in the light of God. Their diseases have challenged them to love their bodies for the first time. Within the equally complicated nature of relationships, we are called to embrace and surround with divine light even those members who create dissension and conflict. Such love may, at times, be "tough love," but its aim is always healing, reconciliation, and alignment with God's will for the body as a whole. This inclusive, yet strong, love was embodied by Abraham Lincoln at the end of the Civil War. When asked how he would treat the defeated South, his companion expected Lincoln to speak of vengeance and humiliation. To his companion's surprise, Lincoln responded, "I'll treat them as if they never had left." Today in South Africa, Desmond Tutu and Nelson Mandela have embodied a love that seeks reconciliation between the Afrikaners and those they once oppressed. This strong love, which brings unity and health to the body, is described by Martin Luther King, Jr.:

> When I speak of love I am not speaking of some sentimental and weak response. I am speaking of that force which all the great religions have seen as the supreme unifying principle of life. Love is somehow the key that unlocks the door which leads to ultimate reality. This Hindu-Moslem-Christian-Jewish-Buddhist belief about ultimate reality is beautifully summed up in the

first epistle of St. John: "Let us love one another; for love is born of God and everyone who loveth is born of God and knoweth God."[2]

Only the Spirit's love can break what King described as the "chain of hate" and bring healing where once there was enmity.

Where the Spirit is present—and the Spirit is present everywhere—there is love. When we proclaim with heart and mind, "I am part of the body of Christ" and then turn to our neighbors with that same affirmation, "You are part of the body of Christ," we will discover our true reality as holy and interrelated. As we claim our places as partners in Christ's body, the world will know that we are Christians by our love.

> We are one in the Spirit, we are one in the Lord,
> we are one in the Spirit, we are one in the Lord,
> and we pray that all unity may one day be restored:
> And they'll know we are Christians by our love, by our love,
> yes, they'll know we are Christians by our love.
>
> PETER SCHOLTES, "THEY'LL KNOW WE ARE CHRISTIANS"

EXERCISE ONE: LIVING BY YOUR AFFIRMATIONS

In this section, we affirm regularly, "I am part of the body of Christ," as we remember our connectedness to all things. To concretize this affirmation, reflect on ways that this affirmation of unity is reflected in your everyday experience. In my own life, I affirm: "I am part of the body of Christ; *I share my love with my family.*" "I am part of the body of Christ; *I reach out to my colleagues in love.*" "I am part of the body of Christ; *I give love to and receive love from everyone I meet.*"

As you experience your relatedness to everyone in the body of Christ, personalize your own affirmations in the following ways:

I am part of the body of Christ; _____.
I am part of the body of Christ; _____.
I am part of the body of Christ; _____.
I am part of the body of Christ; _____.

EXERCISE TWO: LIVING BY YOUR IMAGINATION

After spending some time quietly reflecting on the body of Christ, image your immediate relationships as part of a well-functioning organism. Experience the mind of Christ—the light of Christ—flowing through every cell in this body. Visualize your own place in the body. With what type of cell or organ would you associate yourself within this body? What gifts do you bring to the body? As you reflect on your own gifts for the body, visualize the light of Christ flowing through you, enhancing your personal gifts for your life and for the other parts of the body.

Take time to look at the cells and organs that surround your own part of the body. Experience the gifts of others enhancing your own life. See the whole body as one functioning organism, guided and empowered by the mind of Christ.

As you conclude this meditation, take time to be thankful for the spirit of Christ giving life to you. Visualize those who are enriching your life, both near and far, and give thanks for God's energy moving through your own life.

EXERCISE THREE: FAITH IN ACTION

The body of Christ represents the essential unity of all life. Our joys and sorrows shape one another's experience. The health of the whole body depends on the well-being of its parts.

As you ponder the meaning of the body of Christ, what parts of the body are hurting in your world? How does their brokenness shape your life? How does their pain shape your community?

As you awaken to the wounded parts of the body of Christ, make a commitment to contribute to the well-being of these wounded parts by supporting legislation that encourages education, justice, hunger relief, and appropriate medical care. Take time to see everyone as connected with your life. Treat everyone you meet as a partner in the body of Christ.

Within the Christian life, all prayer is "body prayer," which joins our personal quests for wholeness with the well-being of the persons around us. Commit yourself to interceding on behalf of the poor and neglected persons in your community and the world. Then, to embody your prayers, put your body on the line through acts of loving service. By your love of the whole body, you may become the embodiment of Christ for those who are in pain and despair.

Nothing Is Unclean to Me

The next day, as they [the men from Cornelius' house]
were on their journey and approaching the city, Peter
went up on the roof to pray. He became hungry and
wanted something to eat; and while it was being prepared,
he fell into a trance. He saw the heaven opened and
something like a large sheet coming down, being lowered
to the ground by its four corners. In it were all kinds of
four-footed creatures and reptiles and birds of the air.
Then he heard a voice saying, "Get up, Peter; kill and
eat." But Peter said, "By no means, Lord; for I have never
eaten anything that is profane or unclean." The voice said
to him again, a second time, "What God has made clean,
you must not call profane."

ACTS 10:9–15

Throughout the history of religious experience there has been a battle between religion and spirituality. Today, indeed, many people would confess that they are spiritual but not religious. Whereas I believe that religion—the rituals, structures, and traditions of an institution—and spirituality—the vital, unbridled experience of the Divine—are polarities that complement each other, tragically, however, they are all too often in deadly opposition.

Peter's dream portrays the battle between religion and spirituality in terms of our acceptance of the stranger and outsider. Religion, left to itself, is the sanction of rules, structures, and doctrines. It clearly defines who is a Christian and who is not. It clearly identifies the circle of salvation and place of revelation. Within the walls of religion there are special persons and special revelations that clearly articulate the identity of the believer and, accordingly, disenfranchise the nonbeliever. Certain places and persons are deemed holy, while others are determined to be unholy and godforsaken. In the unfortunate words of a church father, "Outside the church there is no salvation." Historically, this circle of salvation is defined in terms of the belief systems and rituals of well-defined groups, whether they be Roman Catholic, Protestant, or Orthodox Christian. Such religions supply a clear identity and a set of norms, but this clarity

133

is often bought at the price of inflexibility and emphasis on rules rather than persons. In the language of the Protestant Reformation and the twentieth-century theologian Karl Barth, religion—without the lively and iconoclastic presence of spirituality—is works righteousness, the human effort to earn salvation and control God by clearly defined rules, behaviors, and beliefs.

The Spirit is always threatening to the static and inflexible structures of religion. The Spirit blows where it wills and often appears chaotic to those whose faith centers around absolutes; however, the gift of the Spirit is inclusiveness, new life, innovation, and conversion. Tolstoy's Grand Inquisitor from the *Brothers Karamazov* fears the freedom of the Spirit. When Jesus returns to earth, the Christian Grand Inquisitor arrests the One in whom he believes, because he believes that the structures and security of the Christian religion cannot afford the iconoclastic Christ. The freedom of the spirit of Christ is too risky to be permitted free rein.

The movements of the Spirit threaten every inflexible structure. The Spirit welcomes the sinner and the outcast, the enemy and the antagonist. For the Spirit, all places are holy. Even though some moments (for example, the incarnation and resurrection of Jesus) are intensifications of the Spirit's presence, all moments and persons may become manifestations of the Spirit. Ideally, in the life of faith, we integrate within our religious institutions the freedom of the Spirit and the structure of tradition. Both are necessary for the ongoing affirmation of faith. Traditions and persons alike need a center and an identity, but this self-identity must always be subordinate in the life of the Spirit to transformation and love.

Prior to his visionary experience, Peter was sure about the rules. He knew that, as a Jew, he was obliged to avoid eating certain foods and coming into contact with certain persons. These "holiness rules" served a significant purpose in the faith of Peter and his fellow Jews—they provided a sense of self-identity in a contradictory world. But God asks Peter to go beyond his previous self-understanding. "Call nothing unclean," the Lord commands an inflexible Peter. The issue here is not that of diet but of persons. Within the body of Christ, all are welcome and all have a home. There are no second-class citizens, as the apostle Paul asserted in his letter to the Galatians. All are welcome at God's table. Before the Spirit of Christ, all the barriers are broken down: "As many of you as were baptized into Christ have clothed yourselves with Christ. There is no longer Jew or Greek, there is no longer slave or free, there is no longer male and female; for all of you are one in Christ Jesus" (3:27–28).

The freedom of the Spirit does not, as Paul later notes in Galatians, destroy ethics and self-identity. Rather, it always drives us beyond our own personal or theological comfort zones toward the forms of love that are healing in our time. Our freedom in Christ is reflected through love and service. In this Spirit, the self-affirmation of denominational, experiential, or theological traditions can be a healthy phenomenon, a reflection of the diverse encounters with God and an open door to seekers of all kinds, provided it is not used as a tool of exclusion, superiority, or judgment.

What is unclean to you? For many of us, the unclean is not necessarily the alcoholic, homeless person, or foreigner. Instead, for many mainline or liberal Christians, those whom we define as beyond the circle of love may be scientific creationists and members of the Christian coalition, white supremacists, and often fundamentalists, TV evangelists, and those who oppose women's ordination. Who are the people whose message *you* immediately "turn off" or whose needs you immediately "turn from"? These are your unclean persons. Like Peter, we all need the conversion of heart that opens us to God's presence in the least likely places. The Spirit blows where she wills and embraces whomever she desires.

> In Christ there is no east or west, in him no south or north,
> but one community of love throughout the whole wide earth.
>
> In Christ shall true hearts ev'rywhere their high communion find;
> his service is the golden cord, close-binding humankind.
>
> Join hands, disciples of the faith, whate'er your race may be;
> all children of the living God are surely kin to me.
>
> In Christ now meet both east and west in him meet south and north;
> all loving hearts are one in him throughout the whole wide earth.
>
> JOHN OXENHAM, "IN CHRIST THERE IS NO EAST OR WEST"

EXERCISE ONE: LIVING BY YOUR AFFIRMATIONS

The spirit of Christ calls us to see our world with new eyes and new hearts. As we examine our hearts, we are challenged to ponder our own images of uncleanliness. Take time to repeat the affirmation "In Christ, nothing is unclean to me." To personalize it, you may choose to include those whom you initially consider unclean or beyond your care. As you name them, invite God to transform your heart. While you still may challenge the viewpoints and actions of these persons, let your challenge be grounded in love and not fear, defensiveness, or superiority. If God is the circle whose center is everywhere and circumference nowhere, then they too dwell within the circle of God's love.

In my own life, I personalize this affirmation with the following words: "In Christ, *the homeless alcoholic* is not unclean to me." "In Christ, *the person whom I cannot get along with* is not unclean to me." "In Christ, *the Republicans who voted against the nuclear test ban treaty* are not unclean to me."

How would you personalize this affirmation?

In Christ, _____ is (are) not unclean to me.
In Christ, _____ is (are) not unclean to me.
In Christ, _____ is (are) not unclean to me.
In Christ, _____ is (are) not unclean to me.

EXERCISE TWO: LIVING BY YOUR IMAGINATION

In the quiet, visualize yourself in Peter's shoes. You have just taken some time off to relax between meetings. Where are you going to relax? What is it like to take some time off?

In the quiet, you doze off. You see all sorts of creatures, persons, and groups coming toward you, looking for your acceptance and support. Which ones (be honest with yourself) fill you with discomfort, anxiety, or nervousness? Which ones seem to be antagonistic or misguided in their approach toward you or the things you believe in? Which ones are beyond the circle of your love?

As you note the unclean creatures, you hear a voice resounding all around you. This voice pronounces all that you have called unclean to be worthy of love. When you protest that these creatures are unclean and foreign to you, God gives you the vision of each one of them surrounded by a divine light and cleansed by the divine Spirit.

What action do you feel called to take in light of God's care for these formerly unclean beings? How are you called to respond to them?

Following this guided visualization, you might choose to fill in the blanks of Galatians 3:28 with your own list of unwanted characters or social antagonists.

In Christ, there is no longer _____ or _____,
there is no longer _____ or _____,
there is no longer _____ or _____,
for all of you are one in Christ Jesus.

EXERCISE THREE: FAITH IN ACTION

The embodiment of this affirmation is challenging because it calls us to reach out to persons who differ radically from ourselves in politics, theology, personality type, sexual orientation, lifestyle, ethnicity, and so on. Beginning slowly, take time to

(1) Commit yourself to building bridges to the "other" by your words and actions.

(2) Challenge any preconceptions you have about your "particular other." Withdraw any negative projections so that you can see that person as he or she really is.

(3) Examine your speech to eliminate any negative comments about the "other." In times of disagreement, speak the truth as you experience it without bringing in personal judgments.

(4) Find areas of common cause with the "other." For example, anti-abortion and pro-choice persons can unite to encourage appropriate sex education and government/community support for unwed mothers and unwanted children. The point here is to look for areas of deep common affirmation, beneath the rhetoric and projections.

I See God's Presence in "the Least of These"

> *Then the king will say to those at his right hand, "Come,*
> *you that are blessed by my Father, inherit the kingdom*
> *prepared for you from the foundation of the world; for I*
> *was hungry and you gave me food, I was thirsty and you*
> *gave me something to drink, I was a stranger and you*
> *welcomed me, I was naked and you gave me clothing, I*
> *was sick and you took care of me, I was in prison and*
> *you visited me." Then the righteous will answer him,*
> *"Lord, when was it that we saw you hungry and gave you*
> *food, or thirsty and gave you something to drink? And*
> *when was it that we saw you a stranger and welcomed*
> *you, or naked and gave you clothing? And when was it*
> *that we saw you sick or in prison and visited you?" And*
> *the king will answer them, "Truly I tell you, just as you*
> *did it to one of the least of these who are members of my*
> *family, you did it to me."*
>
> MATTHEW 25:34–40

When and where do you see God? Leo Tolstoy tells the story of a humble shoemaker named Martin. A widower who lived by himself in the basement of a building, he could identify the people of his town by the shoes they wore as they passed by his basement window. One evening, he had a dream in which Jesus came to him: "Tomorrow," the Master said, "I will come to visit you." Martin woke in great expectation and began his daily work with eyes wide open to Christ's presence. In the midst of his morning task, he saw the scuffed and well-worn boots of a retired soldier staggering in front of his window. He hailed the elderly man and invited him in for tea and a biscuit on the cold winter's day. A few hours later, he saw a scuffle in front of his window. A young boy had been apprehended for stealing an apple. Just as the merchant was about to take the boy to jail, Martin emerged from his basement and purchased the fruit for the hungry child. As night fell and the winds whipped into a frenzy, he saw the feet of a young woman, weary from a day's journey. He invited her and her young child into the house for hot tea and shelter on their way to the house of her husband's parents, where she would live while her husband was stationed at a distant military post. As she departed, he gave her his wife's shawl to protect her and her baby against the chill winter wind.

As night fell, Martin felt discouraged. He had looked for Jesus all day, but no vision or guest had come to him. As he closed his Bible, he asked Jesus, "Where were you today? You said that you would visit me." Then, in the shadows, he saw three pictures—an old soldier, a young boy, and a mother and child—and heard those ancient words, "As you have done unto the least of these, you have done unto me."

Christ comes to us in every encounter. The light of the world that shines in all things radiates from every heart. This is a matter of reality as well as perception. Divine omnipresence affirms that God's life is the deepest life of all things and that God is present, even when not experienced, in every person and event of our lives. In real life, however, many of us are "practical Gnostics." We reserve God's presence and revelation only for special persons and places—Jesus of Nazareth, a guru, a spiritual teacher, a holy book. Although the message of the incarnation is that God's presence is more vital and healing in some places and persons than others, no place is godforsaken, no person bereft of insight. Although the inner light may be hidden from our perception or the experience of our companions, God's inner light awaits discovery in all things.

In Matthew 25, God comes to the faithful anonymously. Revelation comes in the everyday and the ordinary, and even the repulsive. This was the discovery of Saint Francis. Initially repulsed by the scabrous visages of lepers, he asked God to create in him a new heart and holy vision that would enable him to love the lepers as God's revelation to him. By God's grace, Francis found a new vision that opened his eyes to God's presence in "the least of these," poor and sick humanity, but also the world of Brother Wolf and the birds of the air. The sun, moon, birds, wolves, and fish all spoke forth the revelations of God. Empowered by a new vision of reality, Saint Francis lived by the affirmation "Lord, make me an instrument of your peace."

The spirit of Christ speaks forth in all things. We receive Christ in every encounter. But more importantly, we respond to Christ in every encounter. Our worship of God is manifest in songs of praise and prayers of adoration, but it is also manifest in the gift of "random acts of kindness and simple acts of beauty." Our lives—our love for the least of these— shape the quality of God's own experience. What we do in our everyday as well as political lives makes a difference to God's experience of pain or beauty. In loving creation, God's love flows through us and back into God's own reality.

The passage from Matthew 25 challenges us to see our relationship with God as social as well as personal. What our governments do can add either joy or sorrow to the lives of humankind. We are called to enhance the "life, liberty, and happiness," in the deepest sense, of all humankind by one-to-one actions and political involvement. The faces of "the least of these" come before us as we watch congressional proceedings on C-SPAN or the evening news, in our phone calls to our representatives, in signing petitions, and in our willingness to choose life in our political lives. In a process-relational universe, all spirituality integrates social and personal, political and pastoral, as the gift of our lives to God's life.

> Where cross the crowded ways of life,
> where sound the cries of clan and race,
> above the noise of selfish strife,
> O Christ, we hear your voice of grace.
>
> In haunts of wretchedness and need,
> on shadowed thresholds fraught with fears,
> from paths where hide the lures of greed,
> we catch the vision of your tears.
>
> From tender childhood's helplessness,
> from human grief and burdened toil,
> from famished souls, from sorrow's stress,
> your heart has never known recoil.
>
> The cup of water given for you
> still holds the freshness of your grace;
> yet long these multitudes to view
> the strong compassion in your face.
>
> O Savior, from the mountainside,
> make haste to heal these hearts of pain;
> among these restless throngs abide;
> O, tread the city's streets again.

FRANK MASON NORTH, "WHERE CROSS THE CROWDED WAYS OF LIFE"

EXERCISE ONE: LIVING BY YOUR AFFIRMATIONS

For this affirmation, take time to repeat, "I see God's presence in the least of these." To personalize this, I have used affirmations such as: "I see God's presence in *this homeless person.*" "I see God's presence in *the substance abuser.*" "I see God's presence in *the person who is antagonistic toward me.*"

Where are the least likely places for you to see God's presence? You may choose to place a name in the blank:

I see God's presence in _____.
I see God's presence in _____.
I see God's presence in _____.
I see God's presence in _____.

EXERCISE TWO: LIVING BY YOUR IMAGINATION

Take time to relax in the silence. Let your mind wander through the previous day or week. Which persons during that time seemed especially alien to you? Which persons were a source of discomfort or anger? Which persons did you most wish to avoid? Visualize each of these persons. Look deeply into their lives. Hear Jesus say to you, "As you have done unto the least of these, you have done unto me."

Now look at these persons from a different perspective. See each one of them as Christ sees them. See them as "clothed" in Christ, as reflecting Christ's own presence. Visualize yourself responding to each one of them in the future as if you were responding to Christ.

EXERCISE THREE: FAITH IN ACTION

Christ transforms us by renewing our minds. Experience the spirit of Christ working in your life as you reflect on the least of these. When you think of the "least of these," commit yourself to praying for them. Let your prayers lead you to creative action on their behalf.

Where is God leading you in relation to these persons? Often, the "least of these" are victims of our economic or political systems. What changes in our country would enable these persons to live fuller and happier lives? How can you influence the political system to change their lives for the best? What political action can you involve yourself in?

Responding to the "least of these" often requires hands-on care. Who is forgotten in your church? How can you give them hospitality? Who is forgotten in your family? How can you give them a place of welcome? Who is forgotten in your local community? Where can you reach out to them? As I noted earlier, you might choose to volunteer for a local program such as Habitat for Humanity, a women's shelter, a child tutoring center, or a soup kitchen.

In your family or church, you might choose to write a note, make a phone call, or invite the forgotten one for coffee or lunch. Remember that we are all in this together. There is no "us" and "them." We are all part of the body of Christ. Indeed, much to our surprise, someone may see us as alien or unworthy, as "the least of these." But to someone else in need, we may be a face of Christ, an answer to her or his deepest prayer.

CHAPTER FIVE

Healing and Wholeness in Life and Death

Death confronts us with many faces. As the necessary by-product of change and transformation, images of death surface whenever we are forced to let go of the familiar and stable anchors of our lives. The philosopher Alfred North Whitehead suggests that the experiences of death and loss are constant metaphysical realities. In the spirit of Martin Luther's assertion that "in the midst of life, we are surrounded by death," Whitehead notes that the greatest and most inevitable metaphysical evil is the "perpetually perishing" nature of life. We must let go of the past in order to make way for the immediacy of the present moment. Our lives are filled with "mini" and "many" deaths long before we must face the end of our biological existence.[1]

The shadow of death hovers over even our most joyful celebrations. A couple vows to be faithful to each other "in sickness and in health" and "for as long as we both shall live." But as C. S. Lewis notes, every good marriage ends at the graveside. Death is a natural season of love. Just as marriage follows courtship, death follows the autumn of marital life. Regardless of our medical technology or spiritual evolution, the mortality rate still remains at 100 percent.

The biblical tradition sees death as spiritual and emotional as well as biological, and never entirely as "natural." Things are never quite so simple as Leo Buscaglia's naturalistic meditation on death, *The Fall of Freddie the Leaf.* Along with Dylan Thomas, we "rage against the dying of the light" precisely because our own lives and the lives of those we love hover between the infinite and finite. As Ernest Becker notes in *The Denial of Death,* we are "gods who must die." The ultimate horizon of death conditions every human endeavor. As psychiatrist Robert Jay Lifton asserts, we seek immortality through having children, creating works of art, writing publications, and influencing our children and friends, as well as through mystical experiences and theological doctrines. But all of this will eventually pass. The countries and causes we die for are finite and mortal. The planet whose rainforests and oceans we strive to preserve will eventually perish in a solar explosion. Yet within our world of constant change and transformation, we seek something that endures. We hope that God will remember us, and we pray that death is not the final word of our own personal human adventure. Along with the philosopher Whitehead, we embrace creativity yet yearn for the immortality described by a famous hymn:

> Abide with me; fast falls the eventide;
> the darkness deepens, God, with me abide;
> when other helpers fail, and comforts flee,
> Help of the helpless, O abide with me.
>
> Swift to its close ebbs out life's little day;
> earth's joys grow dim; its glories pass away;
> change and decay in all around I see;
> O thou who changest not, abide with me.
>
> HENRY F. LYTE, "ABIDE WITH ME"

In order to respond creatively to the perpetual perishing of life, we need to discover something that is constant and enduring amid every change.

The sting of death does not trouble the world-denying spirit, whose one goal is to flee from this vale of tears in order to unite eternally as "the Alone to the Alone." Nor does the reality of death trouble those Christians whose faith is grounded in their hope for a divine "rescue mission," a "rapture" that will deliver the saved from this sinful world. But the sting of death torments those of us who love this world deeply through our love of our children and spouses, woodlands and oceans, books and paintings, music and holidays. Now, in my late forties, I ponder the day when my son will look solicitously at me the way I now look solicitously at my ninety-year-old father. I reflect on how quickly my own child has grown from a newborn and a toddler on my knee to a college student who towers over me. I worry about the possibility of a debilitating illness that would rob me of the joys of reading, hiking, eating, and friendship.

Life is indeed a process of perpetual perishing. Although the process of letting go enables us to experience new realities and actualize creative possibilities, eventually we must let go of everything we love. Although we can forestall aging, we cannot ultimately avoid it. The Olympic athlete, almost godlike in her prowess, now stricken with emphysema cannot even walk to the bathroom unaided. The once vibrant music and film idol dies of progressive heart failure in his eighties. The rock star overdoses on heroin. The former president of the United States, who once held the world's fate in his hands as he battled the "evil empire," no longer knows his wife or children due to the onset of Alzheimer's disease.

There would be no "good news" if we were merely passive victims of aging, sickness, and death. If death has the final word spiritually, emotionally, and physically, then our lives would be little more than "a tale told by an idiot, signifying nothing." Amid the powers of darkness, Christian faith boldly affirms an alternative vision of reality that embraces change yet affirms eternal life. The message of the cross and the resurrection proclaims that death is overcome not by avoiding it, repressing it, or choosing to dim the passions of life, but by journeying through the valley of the shadow of death with the living God as our companion. At the heart of a process-relational spirituality is the confident affirmation that death cannot conquer life and that we are held in God's loving care regardless of life's inevitable crises.

Death confronts us in many ways, but three ways seem to be primary: (1) in the debilitating impact of disease and aging, (2) in the inevitable experiences of bereavement and loss, and (3) in our own mortality. The reality of a chronic, intermittent, or terminal illness can deaden the spirit and destroy the flesh. As secure as we may feel in our current health situations, visions of debilitation through heart disease, stroke, cancer, and Alzheimer's disease remind us of our essential physical vulnerability. In light of the reality of disease, Christian faith affirms that the One who brings us salvation was, first and foremost, a healer of body, mind, and spirit. Jesus confronted the many faces of death embodied in chronic illnesses such as leprosy, hemorrhages, and blindness; in grief over the death of friends and followers; and in his own anxiety over humiliation and pain as he turned his face toward Calvary. Among the great religious leaders of humankind, Christ alone placed physical healing at the heart of his ministry. Nearly one-fifth of the gospel stories relate to Jesus' healing ministry. Jesus contended against disease because disease isolates, dominates, and destroys the human spirit. Jesus knew that disease is never just a physical issue but an ever-present reminder of our vulnerability and mortality. The One who sought abundant life challenged anything that rendered human life defenseless and alone.[2]

In the inevitable experience of bereavement, we mourn the loss of the "real presence" of those we have loved. In the wake of a loved one's death, even happy memories cannot replace the sound of her voice or the touch of his hand. Recently, I spoke at the funeral of a dear friend who committed suicide. Her death has diminished my life and the lives of her son and siblings. Nearly every day, I grieve in small ways the deaths of the elders in my life. A few weeks ago, a dear lady from my father's church died at the age of ninety-four. I mourn her passing as I remember her kindness to me when I was a long-haired teenager. When I see old photographs of my family, I still mourn the fact that I am a middle-aged, motherless child. I anticipate the grief that I will experience when my father dies, even though his death is not apparently imminent. When a spouse or friend dies, our hearts are broken and our spirits rent asunder. In our grief, we need the comfort of the One to whom all hearts are open and all desires known. We need an eternity for those we love as much as we do for ourselves. His one wild and precious life cannot forever be lost. Her mortal vibrancy must find an eternal home in the life of God and in a future adventure. While some persons ridicule the images of family reunions on the other side, we all need to believe in further adventures of forgiveness and intimacy with those we love. The unfinished possibilities in ourselves and our loved ones must somehow find wholeness and completion. The image of the heavenly "communion of saints" gives us the vision of a "tender care that nothing be lost" that is worth saving in ourselves and those we love.

Finally, our own mortality speaks constantly to us in deep whispers. Paul Tillich's "ontological shock of non-being" reminds of us of the abyss from which we came, the brief flickering light of this lifetime, and the darkness toward which our lives must fly. We need a vision of everlasting life as we face that life's descending edges. We need the hope of further growth and transformation in the afterlife. We need the assurance that our dying breath will merge with a new life-giving breath as we take the next steps of our spiritual adventure. We need the confidence that the God who loved us into life will receive us in death.

The Christian affirmation of Christ's resurrection affirms that death can only be conquered by facing it directly. Along with Luther, Christian faith asserts, "In the midst of death, we are surrounded by life." The cruciform nature of our faith proclaims that God bears the burden of death in the dying and rising of each moment of our lives, including the "last." The cross of Jesus is a metaphysical as well as historical reality, for God is "the fellow sufferer who understands." Our pain is God's pain. But within the destructive experiences of pain and death, there is also the divine process of transformation. Along with the first Christians, we affirm that the the tomb is empty, death has been defeated, and "Christ is risen." Christ's resurrection is the deepest reality of all things and not merely a historical event in ancient Judea. The One who shares our suffering gives us new life and revives that which is dead in ourselves and our loved ones. The mystery of the resurrection is that wounded love is always stronger than frightening death. For those who have experienced the resurrection, even the crosses of suffering and humiliation can be the doorways into new life.

In the affirmations for this section, we will confront the realities of death, illness, and bereavement in light of the deeper realities of God's creative transformation and everlasting love.

As we live by our affirmations, we will discover that God's healing love is our companion at every stage of our life's adventure and that God has a future planned for us and those we love even beyond the grave.

I Want to Be Healed

> Now in Jerusalem by the Sheep Gate there is a pool,
> called in Hebrew Beth-zatha, which has five porticoes. In
> these lay many invalids—blind, lame, and paralyzed. One
> man was there who had been ill for thirty-eight years.
> When Jesus saw him lying there and knew that he had
> been there a long time, he said to him, "Do you want to be
> made well?" The sick man answered him, "Sir, I have no
> one to put me into the pool when the water is stirred up;
> and while I am making my way, someone else steps down
> ahead of me." Jesus said to him, "Stand up, take your mat
> and walk." At once the man was made well, and he took
> up his mat and began to walk.

JOHN 5:2–9

Do you want to be healed? The answer ought to be obvious. Doesn't everyone want to be healed, after all? But the answer is not absolutely clear, either for ourselves or for the man at the pool. Although he had spent nearly forty years among the sick at the pool, the man's response to Jesus is ambiguous. Much to our surprise, he doesn't say yes. He gives an excuse for his continuing debilitation: "Nobody helps me. Somebody always gets there first when the angel stirs the water."

Ironically, some persons find disease and debilitation advantageous. Early in life every child learns how to manipulate her or his parents with the complaint of a stomachache or a sore throat. When we are sick, we let other persons take care of us. We don't need to take responsibility for our own lives. We can opt out of conflict situations and avoid life's most challenging tests. There is even a familiarity to disease: Our complaints and aches and pains are old friends. Our troubles and complaints often become the core of our identity. Who would we be without them? Although not all disease is chosen consciously or unconsciously, it is clear that the man at the pool was spiritually as well as physically sick.

There are also significant disadvantages to sickness. When we are sick, we are consigned to the sidelines. Our world shrinks to the size of our hospital room or the self-imposed limits we have placed on ourselves.

In our fixation on illness, we fail to grasp our full potential for creativity and relationship.

Jesus did not blame the man for his passivity or debilitation. Although he recognized the psychosomatic nature of the man's illness, Jesus accepted him in spite of his negative thinking. He called him to a new reality and self-understanding. Jesus simply looks at him and challenges him to embrace the healing that is within his reach, "Stand up, take your mat and walk."

Despite his years of debilitation, the man took a chance on Jesus. For a moment, he broke the chains of negativity and illness. Before he stood up on the outside, the man first had to stand up on the inside. He had to say yes to Jesus' vision of health and healing. He had to claim God's creative and healing aim for his life, not in some abstract future but in the concrete moment.

Clearly, our healing has to be "won" moment by moment. Sociologists of medicine distinguish between "curing" and "healing." Curing relates to the cessation of physical symptoms, while healing encompasses our whole being. Healing involves the spiritual renewal and transformation that enables us to live creatively with both health and disease. Initially, the man by the pool is cured but not fully healed, for when the Pharisees ask why he is carrying a mat on the Sabbath, he blames Jesus. "That man made me do it," he exclaims, even though it had truly been his choice to stand up and walk. This may explain Jesus' mysterious admonition to the man: "See, you have been made well! Do not sin anymore, so that nothing worse happens to you." In order to be fully healed, this man needed to affirm his healing, moment by moment and day by day.

Beyond our own resistance to change and our attachment to familiar limitations, God calls each one of us forward into a new and healthy life. Like a good parent, God invites us to stand on our own feet and embrace the new creation. God asks each of us at every moment, "Do you want to be healed? Do you want to stand up? Do you want to claim the adventure of love and life I have planned for you?"

As we explore our own desires for the healing of body, mind, and spirit, we must make our own inner affirmation of faith. We must "stand up" on the inside and say, "I want to be healed! I want to accept God's promise of salvation, of wholeness *today!*" For those who have said yes to God's healing touch, there is no turning back.

I have decided to follow Jesus,
I have decided to follow Jesus,

I have decided to follow Jesus—
no turning back, no turning back.

The world behind me, the cross before me,
the world behind me, the cross before me,
the world behind me, the cross before me—
no turning back, no turning back.

Though none go with me, I still will follow,
though none go with me, I still will follow,
though none go with me, I still will follow—
no turning back, no turning back.

Will you decide now to follow Jesus?
Will you decide now to follow Jesus?
Will you decide now to follow Jesus?—
No turning back, no turning back.

A SONG OF INDIA, "I HAVE DECIDED TO FOLLOW JESUS"

EXERCISE ONE: LIVING BY YOUR AFFIRMATIONS

Do you want to be healed? As you ponder Christ's question to you, make it an affirmation, even if you are still struggling with the choice for new life. "I want to be healed! I want to be healed!" In my own life, I have personalized this affirmation by saying: "I want to be healed of *my shyness among strangers.*" "I want to be healed of *my feelings of negativity.*" "I want to be healed of *my fear of failure.*" "I want to be healed of *my tendency to eat the wrong foods and gain weight.*" An alternative to this might be, "I commit myself to the healing process."

In your own life, where do you see your need of healing? How do you respond to Jesus' question, "Do you want to be healed?"

I want to be healed of _____.
I want to be healed of _____.
I want to be healed of _____.
I want to be healed of _____.

EXERCISE TWO: LIVING BY YOUR IMAGINATION

Today, I invite you to visualize the story of the man at the pool. You are lying at a healing pool, surrounded by sick persons of all kinds. What does the scene look like? Who are your companions? As you sit beside the pool, how are you feeling? What needs healing in your life today? What is immobilizing you? What is preventing you from receiving the healing you need?

As you lie beside the pool, you notice that the healer Jesus is walking toward you. What does Jesus look like? He stops in front of you and fixes his gaze upon you. Visualize Jesus standing beside you. "Do you want to be healed?" Jesus asks. How do you respond to him? Do you respond affirmatively? Do you really want to be healed? What do you need to give up in order to receive your healing? What new adventures will emerge with your healing?

Jesus challenges you to "stand up, take your mat and walk!" With eyes focused on Jesus, visualize yourself gaining confidence and strength as you begin to stand up. You stand up now on your own two feet and go forth cured of your disease. Restored to wholeness, what new possibilities will you now undertake?

Conclude this visualization with a moment of thanksgiving for God's healing presence in your life.

EXERCISE THREE: FAITH IN ACTION

The twelve-step movements assert that in order to be healed, you have to really want it. In one way or another, all of us are limited by past experiences, diseases, or personal brokenness. As you discover the places in your life that are in need of healing and transformation, ask God to give you the strength to choose new life. Insofar as you are able at this moment, commit yourself to the healing process. You can facilitate the healing process in your own life by

(1) joining a support group,

(2) challenging your use of victim language and negative thinking,

(3) claiming what is in your power to change and then committing yourself to it.

The twelve-step movements also maintain that our commitment to personal healing exists alongside our willingness to assist others creatively in their own healing processes. The healing process is profoundly communal and relational in nature. In order to embody this affirmation, you may choose to do one of the following:

(1) Prayerfully support other persons in their need for healing.

(2) Let go of any judgment you may have on those who are struggling with addiction, disease, marital problems. Recognize that each person is carrying a heavy burden and needs your empathy as well as support.

(3) Explore the possibility of initiating a ministry of health and healing in your congregation.

God's Presence Calms My Stress

> *Now as they went on their way, he entered a certain village, where a woman named Martha welcomed him into her home. She had a sister named Mary, who sat at the Lord's feet and listened to what he was saying. But Martha was distracted by her many tasks; so she came to him and asked, "Lord, do you not care that my sister has left me to do all the work by myself? Tell her then to help me." But the Lord answered her, "Martha, Martha, you are worried and distracted by many things; there is need of only one thing. Mary has chosen the better part, which will not be taken away from her."*
>
> LUKE 10:38–42

Today, physicians tell us that our responses to the stresses of life can be hazardous to our health. Unhealthy stress, otherwise known as distress, has been identified with hypertension, depression of the immune system, gastrointestinal problems, arthritis, heart disease, and even acne. Unhealthy stress can damage our relationships, jobs, health, and quality of life.

Just look at your day. How many times do you find yourself on the verge of distress? At the local supermarket, when the line at the check-out stand is moving slowly, shoppers begin to mutter under their breath, tap their fingers, scowl, or even berate the cashier. On the way to work, people often lean on their horns or gesture at the car ahead if it is moving too slowly. Even if we show no outward manifestations of our tension, many of us who live in the affluent West suffer from "hurry sickness" as we rush from one task to another. Others of us are constantly multitasking, living out of multiple centers of awareness as we read the paper, talk on the phone, watch TV, and listen to our children's accounts of the day, all at the same time! By choice or necessity, seldom do we give undivided attention to anything. Even in church, I have seen many people jot down items on a "things to do list" or balance their checkbooks during the pastor's sermon. Rarely are we centered enough to do one thing at a time.

Lest anyone think that I am a curmudgeonly critic of modern technology, I—like virtually everyone in the affluent nations of the world—have benefited from the information and communication revolution of the past few decades. Just yesterday, New Year's Eve, I delighted in being able to follow celebrations of the dawn of the new millennium from the Fiji Islands to San Francisco, all in "real time." Each day, I rejoice in my ability to communicate by e-mail to former students in Romania and England as well as colleagues and friends in Southern California and across town. On a regular basis, I "reach out and touch" my brother in California by phone and my father in a nursing home by fax. I am grateful for the gifts of modern technology, whether in the MRI that detected my son's hidden sinus tumor, the antibiotic that cures an ear infection, or the phone call that brings an invitation to speak at a conference in another state. But I also recognize that stress as a "disease of modern civilization" is primarily an epidemic in the developed countries. Nearly half of our earth's inhabitants have never made or received a telephone call. In our own country, computer literacy among children is closely related to their parents' economic status and level of education.

Stress and distress are a matter of spirit as well as environment. No generation has been bombarded with as many necessities for achieving "the good life." No generation has suffered as much from its own "labor-saving devices" as has our generation. The ambiguity of our technological advances is nowhere more obvious than in the use of the cellular phone, which, on the one hand, enables us to stay in touch with our children, but, on the other hand, is a contributor to automobile accidents, anxiety, and road rage. As a child, I remember hearing on the *Twenty-first Century,* a Sunday evening precursor to *Sixty Minutes,* how much extra time for recreation persons in the 1990s would have. Such prognostications seem sadly simplistic in light of the fact that the average work week and commute time for Americans has actually increased over the years. Indeed, few of us are ever off the job as we constantly attend to "time-saving" cellular phones, e-mail, pagers, fax machines, computers, and voice mail. To neglect one of these items for even a day is to commit a grievous professional and social blunder. While few of us would eliminate these wonders of modern technology, many of us feel painfully aware that we need to move from distraction to mindfulness in our use of technology. As we discover the presence of God in each moment of life, our use of technology will find its true goal—communication, learning, and unity—as a helpful servant rather than an all-consuming and dominating master.

Stress and distress are matters of faith and perception as much as external conflict and pressure. One of the themes of this book is the polarity of abundance and scarcity. Stress is grounded in the perception of scarcity; we are stressed out when we perceive that we don't have enough time, money, energy, wisdom, or control in our lives. But in fact, the more we seek to be in control, the more we become controlled by others. For example, the more you try to control your drive to work, the angrier you become at other drivers. Faith is about letting go and trusting God's abundance, even in the area of time itself.

Healthy stress is essential to growth. Without external and internal challenges, we would remain at a low level of physical, emotional, intellectual, and spiritual achievement. Still, it is easy to succumb to the "Martha syndrome" and think that everything depends on our own efforts. The biblical story is not meant to criticize Martha for her appropriate concern about the welfare of the household. Rather, it points out the dangers of anxiety and distraction. Martha became so distracted in her care-giving that she lost her personal center and became alienated not only from her deepest self, but from her sister and her beloved guest. Martha forgot the one true thing—the purpose of her housecleaning and cooking was to show her love for Jesus. She even snaps at Jesus for allowing Mary to just sit around and soak in his wisdom and love.

Stress-related disease is epidemic in our time. It threatens to overwhelm our spiritual well-being and undermine our health through hypertension, stroke, heart disease, and high cholesterol. The gospel story of the storm at sea is an apt metaphor for the distress that threatens our well-being. With the storms of life surrounding them, the disciples panic and fear for their lives. In the midst of the storm, they become "practical atheists," whose actions and attitudes betray their lack of faith in God. They forget that even as the storm rages, Jesus is with them. When they remember that he is their companion in the storm, both their hearts and the sea itself become calm. Jesus challenges our lack of spiritual centeredness, as he did the disciples during the storm, with the simple question, "Where is your faith?" What do you trust in for your well-being? Do you really believe that God has given you everything you need to be well, prosper, and serve others? Do you trust God amid the challenges and complexities of life?

Yesterday, I had a lively experiment with stress. I had just completed this chapter and was copying it on to a diskette for safekeeping. I inadvertently struck the wrong key, and the whole text disappeared. My elation at completing this book immediately evaporated. For a moment, I felt like throwing my computer out the window. After my wife, Kate, our family's resident computer expert, pronounced my text lost forever, I felt more than a little depressed and angry at myself for not backing up my work more often and at the uncaring exactitude of computer programs. If I were to be true to the affirmative spirit of this book, I would have to re-create this chapter from scratch. After a few moments of prayerful meditation, I took a few breaths, gathered my wits and my notes, and, after looking at my schedule for the next week, realized that although losing the text of this chapter would be a great inconvenience, it would not be a matter of life or death to focus on rewriting it. If I simply disciplined myself each day, I would still have enough time to complete it by early January without overwhelming my mind, body, or spirit. The second effort, as my friend Rev. Patricia Farmer counseled, might even be better than the first.

Where is your faith? We are, with Martha, "worried and distracted by many things." But God invites us to see our lives in a wider perspective. God's abundance is coming to us every moment. God's guidance is revealing to us what is really important in this moment. God's health and vitality is calming our spirits and energizing our lives. In God's presence, we find a center and peace amid the tasks of the day. God beckons us, in our harried days, to find the quiet center—the circle whose center is everywhere and whose circumference is nowhere.

> Come and find the quiet center in the crowded life we lead,
> find the room for hope to enter, find the frame where we are freed:
> clear the chaos and the clutter, clear our eyes, that we can see
> all the things that really matter, be at peace, and simply be.
>
> Silence is a friend who claims us, cools the heat and slows the pace,
> God it is who speaks and names us, knows our being, touches base,
> making space within our thinking, lifting shades to show the sun,
> raising courage when we're shrinking, finding scope for faith begun.
>
> SHIRLEY ERENA MURRAY, "COME AND FIND THE QUIET CENTER"

EXERCISE ONE: LIVING BY YOUR AFFIRMATIONS

In this section, take time to affirm, "God's presence calms my stress," or "God gives me peace today." In my own life, I recently concretized this with regard to my computer mishap: "God's presence gives me peace *while I try to recover my work.*" "God's presence calms my spirit as *I try to re-create this chapter.*" At other times, I have affirmed, "God gives me peace as *I prepare for this very busy day.*"

In what ways do you feel called to personalize this affirmation? Where do you see the stresses of life challenging you today?

God's presence calms my spirit as _____.
God's presence calms my spirit as _____.
God gives me peace as _____.
God gives me peace as _____.

Exercise Two: Living by Your Imagination

In this visualization, let us journey back to Mary and Martha's home to find ourselves amid Martha's struggles.

Take time to be still and know that God is with you. Image yourself preparing for a dinner party. Jesus the healer and teacher, your beloved friend, is coming to join you. Visualize your kitchen. What foods are you preparing for him? How are you preparing the house for his stay?

You look at your watch and realize that Jesus will be arriving soon and you are not yet prepared for his coming. How do you feel as you look at your list of "to do's"? You hear a knock at the door. Your sister, Mary, greets Jesus, but you stay in the kitchen. After all, there is plenty of work to do and so little time in which to do it. You hear Mary and Jesus chatting and laughing as you busy yourself around the kitchen. How do you feel when you contrast your hard work with Mary's joyful conversation?

Jesus comes into the kitchen. You complain, "Make Mary do something. I'm doing all the work." Jesus says nothing. He simply gazes at you with understanding and loving eyes. He speaks your name: "_____, you are worried and distracted by many things."

Now take a moment to pause and ponder all the things in your life that currently are distracting and anxiety-producing. You share your distress with Jesus as you hear his gentle voice of comfort. "Remember, _____, today, only one thing is really important." What is the "one thing" that you need today in order to be centered? What is the most important thing that you need to address with calm and peace today? Share this with Jesus, and receive a blessing on your tasks of the day.

Conclude this meditation with thanksgiving for God's abundance and peace in your life.

As you return to your tasks, remember what is truly important in your life. Remember that God will give you enough time, energy, wisdom, and intelligence to accomplish every task that lies before you.

EXERCISE THREE: FAITH IN ACTION

Although many of us seek to respond to stress, we are equally called to stress prevention. The same practices that reduce stress also prevent it from overwhelming us in the first place.

God created our bodies aiming toward health and well-being. If we follow the simple rules of divine stewardship of our bodies, minds, and spirits, we will experience greater well-being and peace.

Take time each day for quiet prayer. In an earlier chapter, we reviewed "centering prayer" as taught by Basil Pennington and Thomas Keating. If you have not begun a meditative practice, consider once more the daily practice of centering prayer as a means of spiritual growth and stress reduction. I believe that daily quiet time is at the heart of spiritual, physical, and relational well-being. To reiterate the message of an earlier chapter, in the practice of centering prayer, one does the following:

(1)   Find a comfortable place and close your eyes.

(2)   Begin with a prayer of openness to God.

(3)   Focus on your prayer word (such as "peace," "love," "Christ," "God," "Spirit," "light," etc.).

(4)   When distractions occur, gently and without judgment return to your prayer word.

(5)   After 15–20 minutes, close with the Lord's Prayer.

Breath is essential to well-being. When we are under stress, our breath becomes shallow and fast. Take time to connect with God's peace through breath prayer. Let your breaths slow down your emotions and physical tension. Breathe regularly and deeply, opening yourself with each breath to God's peaceful companionship with words such as "I breathe the Spirit deeply in."

Take time to exercise regularly. If you are short of clock time, you can integrate your prayer and exercise by focusing on your breath or prayer word with the rhythm of your walking, running, or swimming. Regular exercise discharges the stresses of life and enhances your immune system.

Take regular times each week for "sabbath time," that is, time set apart for "just being." Because I am tempted to study and write every day, I have chosen to take the period between sunset on Saturday and sunset on Sunday as a weekly "sabbatical." During that time, I focus on prayer, family, and devotional and recreational reading. I do my best to avoid even checking my e-mail messages or doing advance planning in my date book. During what regular times in the course of your week can you take a few hours to "let go and let God" in prayerful re-creation and family life?

Remember that God is always with you and that God will sustain you, especially in those areas where you have the least control. Take time to internalize Reinhold Niebuhr's version of the Serenity Prayer: "God give *me* grace to accept with serenity the things that cannot be changed, courage to change the things that should be changed, and the wisdom to distinguish the one from the other."

My Faith in God Is Making Me Well

> *Now there was a woman who had been suffering from*
> *hemorrhages for twelve years. She had endured much*
> *under many physicians, and had spent all that she had;*
> *and she was no better, but rather grew worse. She had*
> *heard about Jesus, and came up behind him in the crowd*
> *and touched his cloak, for she said, "If I but touch his*
> *clothes, I will be made well." Immediately her hemorrhage*
> *stopped; and she felt in her body that she was healed of*
> *her disease. Immediately aware that power had gone forth*
> *from him, Jesus turned about in the crowd and said,*
> *"Who touched my clothes?" And his disciples said to him,*
> *"You see the crowd pressing in on you; how can you say,*
> *'Who touched me?'" He looked all around to see who had*
> *done it. But the woman, knowing what had happened to*
> *her, came in fear and trembling, fell down before him, and*
> *told him the whole truth. He said to her, "Daughter, your*
> *faith has made you well; go in peace, and be healed of*
> *your disease."*
>
> MARK 5:25–34

Today, physicians and laity alike are recognizing the significance of the "faith factor," the power of faith to heal, in medical practice and patient care. Strongly held beliefs have profound physiological consequences. In both real life and pharmaceutical testing, the "placebo" and "nocebo" effects, that is, the impact of positive and negative thinking on health and illness, are clearly evident. As physician Larry Dossey asserts, our faith can cure or kill us!

The story of the woman healed of a hemorrhage is one of the most beloved healing narratives. Persons who live daily with chronic illness can easily identify with her twelve-year struggle with what scholars suspect to be a gynecological ailment. Day after day she lived with humiliation and uncertainty. In an era before social safety nets and health insurance, she spent virtually all her money searching for a cure. She also suffered from the social alienation of being "unclean."

159

For persons with serious illnesses, time is often measured by scheduled visits to physicians and medical procedures. The world often shrinks to the size of our particular ailments. Our aches and pains, our insecurities about travel, and our worries about the future often dominate our thinking. Even the visits to the doctors provide little relief. The hours spent in the waiting room, the medications with side effects often as debilitating as the illness, the indignity of being treated by physicians and nurses in a perfunctory or condescending manner all take their toll on our mental and physical health.

Philosophers of medicine distinguish between a disease and an illness. A disease is a set of symptoms described by a particular diagnosis such as cancer, heart disease, arthritis, or AIDS. An illness, on the other hand, represents the social and religious meanings of a disease. For example, AIDS—to the fundamentalist preacher—represents God's punishment of homosexuals for their sinfulness. Although they are seldom blamed for their diseases, people with cancer often see death and indignity as their likely future, even though the majority of persons diagnosed with cancer survive. In her culture, the woman with the flow of blood faced the profound moral and spiritual implications of her illness on a daily basis. Because of her continual and unpredictable bleeding, she could not attend temple services because she was considered ritually "unclean." Every chair she sat on and bed she lay on would remain unclean until it was properly cleansed. If she were married, she could not have normal sexual relations with her husband without contaminating him. Further, in the Jewish society of her time, the incidence of disease was identified with sin, whereas health was perceived as an authentic sign of righteousness. No doubt her neighbors suspected her morality. The woman, no doubt, asked herself, "What have I done wrong? Why is God punishing me? What can I do to be healthy again?"

Chronic illness can destroy the spirit, but it can also build character and courage. When she heard that Jesus was coming to her town, the woman was probably ambivalent at first. "Will he fail, too? Will he scorn me as unclean?" But she claimed the courage to seek him out and, heedless of the stares of her neighbors, she pushed her way through the crowd with only one thought on her mind: "If I but touch his garment, I will be healed."

Although disease may dominate our thinking, faith opens us to new possibilities and energies for transformation. Focusing only on Jesus, the woman forgot all about her years of pain and indignity. In her boldness, she violated two social taboos of her people: She touched a man who was not her brother, husband, or father, *and* she risked Jesus' resentment and retaliation because her touch would render *him* ritually unclean. But no such taboo bore any weight with Jesus.

Scripture simply states that a power that went forth from Jesus healed her. While we can only speculate on the nature of this power, it bears a resemblance to the *chi* energy described by Chinese medicine. Aware of the power flowing from him, Jesus asks, "Who touched me?"

Although the disciples think it is foolish, Jesus' question points to the heart of the story. Of the whole crowd, only one person really touched Jesus, and that day, through Jesus, God touched her. Divine power is constantly flowing through the universe. When we open our lives to God's possibilities, this energy flows in and through our lives, giving us new insight, freeing us from emotional bondage, and making us whole.

Jesus says, "Your faith has made you well." This woman with the hemorrhage was cured physically, but she was also healed spiritually. Jesus called her forth, affirmed her free of disease, and transformed her social status from outcast to member. But more than that, Jesus marshaled the faith in God that would transform every aspect of her life from there on out.

In this healing story, we can easily glimpse our own place in God's healing partnership. Two factors were essential for this woman's healing: First, her faith opened her to divine energy and wholeness; second, God's wholeness flowed into her life, making her whole. Although God's graceful care—the divine providence—always precedes our efforts, there are occasions when, without our own efforts, the divine energy will remain dormant.

Today, Jesus speaks to our chronic ailments and to our struggles that go on year after year. To us, Jesus says, "God is working in your life. God's energy surrounds and permeates your whole being. Awaken to new and unexpected possibilities. Son, your faith has made you well; go in peace, be healed of your disease. Daughter, your faith has made you well; go in peace, be healed of your disease."

EXERCISE ONE: LIVING BY YOUR AFFIRMATIONS

There are many variations of this affirmation that you may choose to employ. One may affirm, "My faith in God is making me whole," or "God's energy is flowing through me, bringing health and healing into my life," or "Divine energy is constantly filling me with new life."

I have concretized this affirmation in the following manner: "My faith in God is making me whole *spiritually and physically.*" "My faith in

God *gives me strength to face this situation with courage.*" "God's energy is flowing through me, *giving me health and wholeness in body, mind, and spirit.*" In what ways is this affirmation speaking to you today?

My faith in God is making me whole _____.
God's energy is flowing through me, _____.
My faith in God is making me whole _____.
God's energy is flowing through me, _____.

EXERCISE TWO: LIVING BY YOUR IMAGINATION

In the style of Ignatian spirituality, we will explore the meaning of this affirmation through a guided meditation. In the quiet, reflect on an issue of mind, body, relationship, or spirit that has troubled you for a long time. In what ways has this issue changed your life? How has it diminished your personal and spiritual vitality? How has this issue placed you at life's sidelines?

As you reflect on your personal issues and their impact on your life, you hear that Jesus will soon be coming to your town. How do you feel about his visit? As you look into the distance, you see a large crowd gathering along the roadside. You glimpse Jesus and his disciples walking toward you. You begin to push your way through the crowd with just one thought on your mind: "If I just touch his clothes, I will be well. If I just touch his clothes, I will be well. If I just touch his clothes, I will be well."

As Jesus passes right by you, you reach out and touch him. Power surges from him and envelops your whole being. You feel transformed and re-created. Jesus stops suddenly and looks around. "Who touched me?" he asks. You decide to step forward and identify yourself. How do you feel about revealing yourself to Jesus?

Jesus looks straight at you and proclaims, "_____, your faith has made you well; go in peace, you are healed of your disease." How does it feel to hear Jesus say these words to you? Notice today's tension, dis-ease, and mental anxiety drop. Repeat Jesus' affirmation to yourself, "My faith has made me well."

Conclude your time of meditation with a period of thanksgiving for God's healing energy in your life.

EXERCISE THREE: FAITH IN ACTION

Today, many churches are reclaiming the healing ministry of Jesus. There are many liturgical and practical ways that you can increase the partnership of spirituality and health at the parish and community levels:

(1) Encourage your church to initiate a parish nursing program or to explore ways in which a ministry of health advocacy and healing can be integrated into worship and Christian education.

(2) Encourage your church to begin a Bible study on the healings of Jesus.

(3) If there is sufficient interest, support the initiation of a liturgical healing service at your church. This can either be facilitated in the context of the primary Sunday worship service or at a special service, weekly or monthly.

(4) As you nurture the healing of persons in your church, remember that healing and health are social as well as personal issues. A person's well-being is determined, in part, by economics, education, and accessibility. Advocate for a just and universal health care policy.

Take time to research the various modalities of holistic medicine in conjunction with your research on the healings of Jesus. Today, many Christians are exploring forms of energy medicine such as acupuncture, therapeutic touch, and reiki. Do you find any common ground between Jesus' healing ministry and Chinese medicine and therapeutic touch? As Christians, we believe that the light of God shines on all persons, and that wherever truth is found, God is present, even if the name of Jesus is not explicitly affirmed.

God's Grace Is Sufficient for Me

> *A thorn was given me in the flesh, a messenger of Satan*
> *to torment me, to keep me from being too elated. Three*
> *times I appealed to the Lord about this, that it would*
> *leave me, but he said to me, "My grace is sufficient for*
> *you, for power is made perfect in weakness." So, I will*
> *boast all the more gladly of my weaknesses, so that the*
> *power of Christ may dwell in me. Therefore I am content*
> *with weaknesses, insults, hardships, persecutions, and*
> *calamities for the sake of Christ; for whenever I am weak,*
> *then I am strong.*
>
> 2 CORINTHIANS 12:7–10

Nothing reveals our vulnerability and mortality more directly than chronic, long-term, intractable illnesses of body, mind, and spirit. Day after day and year after year, we search for a solution, a cure, a magic bullet—an antidote to relieve the depression, weakness, obsessive thoughts, panic, and pain. Whereas others glide easily through life, sometimes just answering the phone, driving the car, going out to eat, or climbing steps are a challenge. Often, the glib testimonies of faith healings broadcast by televangelists seem an insult to those whose prayers for relief of body, mind, and spirit go unanswered. These heroic adventurers, who must face chronic illness on a daily basis, must also daily face challenges to their beliefs. Why am I not healed? Is God overlooking me? Did I do something wrong? Why did God cure that person's alcoholism or depression and not my own? Why is God overlooking my Crohn's Disease while another person received God's blessing?

One of the great insights of biomedicine has been its medicalization of many mental and physical challenges that were previously named and blamed only as social stigmas. Whereas the ancients and even some moderns identified depression with laziness, homosexuality with sin, childlessness with divine punishment, modern medicine has relieved persons of the moral burdens of disease. Disease is entirely nonvoluntary and accidental from the moral perspective, asserts modern Western medicine. Although I believe that there is always a spiritual and emotional component in illness that escapes the reductionistic definitions of biomedicine, I affirm the liberating message of modern medicine to persons who suffer from diseases beyond their power to control. Although we are not impotent in our health and well-being, we are also not omnipotent—we do not fully "create our own realities" as new agers suggest, nor are our diseases the result of a lack of faith or disobedience as certain conservative Christians assert. Still, even without the burden of sin and blame, chronic illnesses of mind and body can destroy and embitter all but the most stalwart human spirit.

The gospel is demeaned when it is presented solely in terms of material success and prosperity. Although I believe that our connectedness to God through positive affirmations and prayer awakens us to the inflowing, abundant power of divine energy to transform and cure, one cannot reduce that connection to a simple linear formula. Indeed, the message of the cross proclaims that God is present redemptively even in and through the most debilitating experiences of suffering. If the gospel is to be truly good news, it must address the "failures" as well as the "successes." It must provide a healing word for those who will not get well and who receive no visible cure. To be faithful to the gospel and to those who suffer from chronic illnesses, we must distinguish between the *curing* of physical symptoms and the *healing* of the whole person.

The apostle Paul faced just such an intractable disease. We don't know the nature of his ailment, but it radically shaped his life. Perhaps some of his fellow believers questioned his faith in light of this continuing personal torment. "Didn't you say, 'I can do all things'? Didn't you preach, 'God will supply all your needs'? Where are you going wrong, Paul? What is standing between you and God?" No doubt these same questions plagued the overanalytic and guilt-sensitive apostle himself. Despite his mystical experiences, Paul cannot overcome this "thorn in the flesh." His prayers seem to go unanswered. God seems not to be listening to his desire for personal deliverance.

In the depths of his struggles, Paul hears the word of God: "My grace is sufficient for you. Power is made perfect in weakness." God is with us in our illness. Nothing—not even a thorn in the flesh—can separate us from the love of God in Christ Jesus our Lord. Suffering need not prevent Paul from living faithfully.

Paul's words accentuate the distinction between curing and healing. Paul is healed—his spirit is restored and he finds peace despite his disability—even though he does not receive a cure.

For reasons none of us can fully discern, our prayers for a cure are not always answered. Although God is not responsible for our diseases and distress, I believe that God is with us in the deepest of trials as our companion, guide, and counsel. To proclaim that "in all things, God works for good" is to affirm that there is a divine presence leading us forward, even in the most intractable and unresolved situations. Where there is no cure, there still is companionship and spiritual transformation.

We all need to hear the gospel message addressed to those who do not "succeed" in finding deliverance from painful and chronic illnesses, because eventually all of us encounter a problem beyond our ability to change or avoid. We will all view life from a hospital bed, beside a loved one, or the graveside. We will all face the debilitation of aging or serious illness. In these dark and difficult times, we will need the good news that God is working in our lives, no matter what our outward circumstances. We need to know that God loves us completely and passionately, even in life's darkest moments.

In her *A Ring of Endless Light,* Madeline L'Engle describes a young girl's relationship to her dying grandfather. Although weakened in body and mind by acute leukemia, Vicky's grandfather still feels that he has a vocation. In his weakness, he is still strong, for his task in life is now simply to pray. With this same deep faith, my paralyzed and incontinent father still prays daily for those who must clean, bathe, and move him. He is not alone, for countless people have found that God's intimate grace is sufficient to give them courage and compassion despite illnesses of mind, body, and spirit.

In every situation of life, I believe that God's grace is indeed sufficient. In the darkest valley, there is One walking beside us, providing comfort and courage to face what we cannot change and insight into the gifts that, even in our weakness, we can share with others. Thanks be to God for the Spirit that shares our most difficult journeys.

> Spirit of God, descend upon my heart;
> wean it from earth, through all its pulses move;
> stoop to my weakness, mighty as thou art,
> and make me love thee as I ought to love.
>
> I ask no dream, no prophet ecstasies,
> no sudden rending of the veil of clay,
> no angel visitant, no opening skies,
> but take the dimness of my soul away.
>
> Teach me to feel that thou art always nigh;
> teach me the struggles of the soul to bear:
> to check the rising doubt, the rebel sigh;
> teach me the patience of unanswered prayer.
>
> GEORGE CROLY, "SPIRIT OF GOD, DESCEND UPON MY HEART"

Exercise One: Living by Your Affirmations

To live out this affirmation, take time in any challenging situation to affirm: "God's grace is sufficient for me. God's grace is sufficient for me." We can personalize this in as many ways as there are difficult situations in life. I have concretized this as follows: "God's grace is sufficient for me as *I ponder my vocational future.*" "God's grace is sufficient for me as *I face the challenges of middle age.*" "God's grace is sufficient for me as *I meet with (a difficult person).*"

In what ways do you need to embody God's gracefulness in your own personal challenges?

God's grace is sufficient for me as _____.
God's grace is sufficient for me as _____.
God's grace is sufficient for me as _____.
God's grace is sufficient for me as _____.

Exercise Two: Living by Your Imagination

In a quiet moment, reflect on your own life. What problems are chronic and apparently unresolvable at this time of your life? Visualize them from a variety of angles. How do they disable you? How do they shape your life?

As you reflect on one problem at a time, imagine that God is with you, standing beside you. Note whether the figure you envisage is male or female, young or old, or perhaps a "being of light." Share with God your feelings about each problem. Listen to God respond, "My grace is sufficient for you. My power is made perfect in weakness." Place each problem, one by one, in God's hands. Give God the burdens of fear and impatience. Hear God say to you, "I am with you always."

Reassured by God's presence, listen once more to God's voice in the depths of your soul. Ask for divine insight and courage for dealing with the problems. Do you receive any responses that you can integrate into your life?

Take time to conclude your visualization with a sense of God's constant companionship and a feeling of gratitude for God's love and resourcefulness.

Exercise Three: Faith in Action

In our weaknesses, we are strong, for God's grace is always sufficient for us. In our awareness of God's grace, we are called to affirm this fact to one another. In embodying this affirmation in daily life, we are challenged to understand and reach out to people who are struggling with apparently intractable diseases such as addiction, depression, and panic disorders. First, we are called to withdraw all judgments and accept them as they are. Look at their lives closely. Try to empathize with their experiences. Try to discern the struggles they face daily and the courage they must muster just to get through the day. As you learn to identify with their situations and support them in action, don't forget to take time to surround them with prayers of healing and love.

We need to pray for the broken, but we also need to create a society that provides for their needs. Educate yourself on issues related to mental health, disability, and addiction as well as chronic illness. Support, personally and politically, programs that enable persons to find creative support in facing physical and mental illness. Advocate for a realistic and inclusive program for universal health care in the United States. Explore the resources for persons with chronic and mental illnesses in your community. Encourage your church to become a haven for those who are struggling with lifelong problems. Advocate for strong safety nets of housing, medical care, and counseling for persons struggling with difficult life problems.

God Is Healing My Grief

But we do not want you to be uninformed, brothers and
sisters, about those who have died, so that you may not
grieve as others do who have no hope. For since we
believe that Jesus died and rose again, even so, through
Jesus, God will bring with him those who have died.

1 THESSALONIANS 4:13–14

A story is told of a woman who came to Gautama the Buddha, carrying the corpse of her only son. "Kind teacher, please bring my son back to life," she begged. The Buddha responded affirmatively, "I will restore your son to life. But you must bring me a mustard seed from a home in the nearby village. However, this seed must come from a household that has never buried a parent, child, sibling, grandparent, or beloved animal." Later that day, the woman returned and told the Buddha that she had just left her son at the funeral pyre. She had realized that grief and death were universal, and nothing she could do could prevent her own or her son's eventual demise.

Grief and death are universal, and our responses to the necessary and inevitable losses of life can transform or destroy us. Christianity finds its origins in the death and resurrection of Jesus and the transformation of the disciples from mourners into proclaimers. Buddhism has its origins in the young prince Gautama's realization, following his encounters with a sick man and a corpse, that, despite his wealth and power, he cannot escape the perpetual perishing of life.

Whether or not we have buried a parent or child, we have experienced the pain of grief. Life's perpetual perishing is characterized by a succession of "mini" deaths, some barely noticed, others heart-rending. Think for a moment of the losses that you have experienced in the course of your life: moving, aging, graduation, leaving home for the first time, the empty nest when the children go off to college or get married, divorce, the loss of friends, the loss of a job, the loss of health and vitality. And, eventually, all of us will stand at the graveside or columbarium mourning the death of a spouse, parent, or dear friend.

Grief is the price we pay for having loving relationships. In the chronicle of his experience following his wife's death, *A Grief Observed,*

169

C. S. Lewis asserts that just as marriage follows courtship, bereavement follows every good marriage. How we respond to bereavement can be a matter of life and death. Medical studies note that in the year following the death of a spouse, the surviving spouse is at greater risk of death, disease, and mental illness than during virtually any other time in her or his life. After the death of a child from a prolonged illness such as cancer, it is not unusual for his or her parents to separate or divorce. When a child or spouse dies, a part of ourselves dies as well. Although the wounds of grief always remain, life calls us to begin again, to discover a new self, and to trust in the unseen forces of healing in the midst of our deepest pain.

A creative response to grief and bereavement is grounded in trust in God's healing presence, the support of a loving community, and hope in the possibility of life after death for ourselves and our loved ones. Without the companionship of God, Paul asserts, our grief would be hopeless. In light of the resurrection, God's presence provides us with companionship and hope for the future. On the one hand, God is with us in our sufferings, intimately experiencing our sense of loss and abandonment, yet promising, "Lo, I am with you always." On the other hand, God promises us an "afterlife," first, in terms of the continuing adventures of the one who has died in God's everlasting realm, and, second, in terms of God's faithful presence leading us toward new life and a new self-identity.

Sometimes, in the midst of our deepest grief, we cannot imagine life without the beloved one. Yet God calls us to gently reach out toward the future even as we remember the past. God reminds us that we are stronger than we think we are. The creative transformation of grief is embodied in the widow who returns to college and receives her Ph.D. four years after her husband's death, the parent who commits herself to the crusade against drunk driving following her child's senseless death at the hands of an intoxicated driver, or the widower who learns to cook and writes a book of love poems in the years following his wife's death. Such personal transformation is neither easy nor accidental, but is the gift of a commitment to choose life, to embrace God's possibilities, and to welcome the support of a loving community.

For most persons, grief heals—like a broken bone—at its own gentle pace. The wound of grief always will remain and will be especially noticed at holidays, birthdays, anniversaries, and special places. Still, God's healing power brings new life even to those whose grief is most heartbreaking.

As a holistic phenomenon, grief challenges us emotionally, spiritually, and somatically. Although there is no one pattern to our grief processes, most people experience temporary physical and emotional depression, ambivalence, tears, guilt, denial, shock, anger. For many, Jesus' cry "Why have you forsaken me?" becomes a mantra of divine abandonment. These and other feelings of grief are normal and natural parts of both the deep wound and the process of healing. Indeed, in the days following a loved one's death, many bereaved people feel as if they are going crazy, especially in light of their inability to control their thoughts or emotions. However, if your grief or the grief of another persists or becomes completely debilitating, it is important that you seek assistance from your pastor, a pastoral counselor, or a psychiatrist. There are spiritual, psychological, and medical resources that we can use to respond creatively to the wound of grief.

Paul counsels us to experience our grief in light of God's promise of eternal life for those we love and for ourselves. The apostle Paul does not ask us to deny our grief, but to place it in the loving care of God, who has loved our spouses, children, and friends into life and who has received their spirits in death. In companionship with God, we are called to participate in a great adventure in this life and the next. We hope for a reunion and further growth with those we love in a realm that transcends anything we can imagine from our earthly perspective. "Grieve, but not as those who are hopeless." With hope in God's eternal love, we can embrace our sorrows with gratitude and courage.

Let hope and sorrow now unite
to consecrate life's ending,
and praise good friends now gone from sight,
though grief and loss are rending.
The story in a well-loved face,
the years and days our thoughts retrace,
are treasures worth defending.

With faith, or doubt, or open mind
we whisper life's great question.
The ebb and flow of space and time
surpass our small perception.
Yet knowledge grows with joyful gains
and finds out wonders far more strange
than hopes of resurrection.

Be glad for life, in age or youth;
its worth is past conceiving.
And stand by justice, love, and truth
as patterns for believing.

Give thanks for all each person gives—
as faith comes true, and Jesus lives,
there'll be an end to grieving.

BRIAN WREN, "LET HOPE AND SORROW NOW UNITE"

EXERCISE ONE: LIVING BY YOUR AFFIRMATIONS

Today, take time to reflect on your experiences of loss. Are any of these losses still dominating your emotional or spiritual life? Respond to your experiences of loss with the affirmation "God is healing my grief." I have concretized this affirmation with the words: "God is healing my grief over *the loss of my job.*" "God is healing my grief as *I ponder my father's debilitating illness and eventual death.*" "God is healing my grief as *I face the challenges of midlife.*"

I would note two things briefly here. First, I believe that the "midlife crisis" is a grief experience, involving the loss of youth and infinite possibility, that calls us to spiritual transformation rather than hasty external transformations such as divorce, affairs, and changes of career. Second, the healing of grief is not in denial, but rather in enabling the griever to face fully the pain, knowing that the pain and grief will not overwhelm her or him.

In your own life, what grief experiences are you facing? Take time to personalize this affirmation.

God is healing my grief as _____.
God is healing my grief as _____.
God is healing my grief over _____.
God is healing my grief over _____.

EXERCISE TWO: LIVING BY YOUR IMAGINATION

In the stillness, take time to reflect on the losses you have experienced in your life. Which losses are still fresh in your experience? Which wounds still give you pain from time to time?

Go back in your memory to a particular loss that still shapes your life. Experience the loss in its rawness. How did you feel at the time? What was the most painful aspect of the loss?

Visualize the encounter with loss, including your final words with the one who has died (or at a situation of loss). Do you feel any guilt? Is there anything unfinished in the relationship?

Now, bring Jesus into the scene. Take time to tell Jesus how you are feeling. Share your tears, anger, guilt, and loss with him. Release your grief to Jesus' loving care. Place your feelings in his hands. What does

Jesus say to you? What words of comfort does he give to you? If you feel guilt over the relationship, listen to Jesus say these words to you, "Father, forgive _____. Begin a new life. Become a new creation." Take time to share your experience of forgiveness with Jesus. Conclude by thanking God for the love, companionship, and new life that God is giving you.

EXERCISE THREE: FAITH IN ACTION

In this section, I will be giving some suggestions on how you and your church can reach out to those who grieve.

(1) Initiate a grief support group in your church. These groups provide an opportunity for people to share their feelings and discover that they are not alone in their bereavement. Grief often isolates persons, while the experience of community expands our lives and interests. Suggest that your church provide quarterly grief workshops, with themes such as grief and rituals, relating to children, beginning again, facing anger, and living through the holidays.

(2) Suggest that your church have a holiday service of remembrance a week or so before Christmas. Some churches refer to this as a "blue Sunday" or "blue Christmas" service. This is important, because the first year of holidays following the death of a loved one is often the most difficult.

(3) Following the funeral, we often say to the bereaved, "Call me if you need something." Rather than making someone wait for a call that usually does not come, commit yourself in the year following to supporting the one who is grieving. Take time to call every few weeks, invite him or her out for coffee or tea, volunteer to help with tasks around the house, offer to drive her or him to church. If you perceive any serious problems, contact your pastor or leader of your shepherding or Stephen Ministry group.

(4) Learn as much as you can about the grief experience. Although there are many fine books on the grief process, I would suggest the following: C. S. Lewis, *A Grief Observed;* Victor Parachin, *Grief Relief;* and Granger Westberg, *Good Grief.*

(5) Take time to remember and reach out to the forgotten survivors, especially estranged spouses or homosexuals whose friends or partners have died of AIDS, parents of children who have died of AIDS, and relatives of persons who have committed suicide. Although their feelings of loss may be great, often they are not given permission to grieve their losses in the context of our culture's rituals of grief.

God Is with Me in the Darkest Valley

> The LORD is my shepherd, I shall not want.
> He makes me lie down in green pastures;
> he leads me beside still waters;
> he restores my soul.
> He leads me in right paths
> for his name's sake.
> Even though I walk through the darkest valley,
> I fear no evil;
> for you are with me;
> your rod and your staff—
> they comfort me.
> You prepare a table before me
> in the presence of my enemies;
> you anoint my head with oil;
> my cup overflows.
> Surely goodness and mercy shall follow me
> all the days of my life,
> and I shall dwell in the house of the LORD
> my whole life long.
>
> PSALM 23

The juxtaposition of Psalms 22 and 23 is no accident. Best known as the source of Jesus' words on the cross, "My God, my God, why have you forsaken me?" Psalm 22 portrays the deepest dimensions of human misery. Virtually every form of brokenness is represented within this psalm of lament and petition—the absence of God, alienation, humiliation, physical and mental anguish, oppression, and death. Tormented by the powers of darkness, the psalmist feels totally alone in the universe, betrayed by friends and abandoned by God. In his misery, the psalmist begs for divine acknowledgment and protection. "Do not be far from me, for trouble is near and there is no one to help" (v. 11). His agony is deepened by his remembrance of God's deliverance and intimacy in the past. But still there is hope, for there is an unseen light even in the darkness. Perhaps God will respond and come to his rescue. The deafening silence may give way to a comforting presence. "But you,

O LORD, do not be far away! O my help, come quickly to my aid! Deliver my soul from the sword, my life from the power of the dog! Save me from the mouth of the lion!" (vv. 19–21).

An authentic spirituality must embrace—like the vows of marriage—every season of life. It must provide guidance, comfort, power, and presence in "better or worse, richer or poorer, sickness and health." In her book *Traveling Mercies,* author Anne Lamott notes that religion is for persons who are afraid of going to hell, whereas spirituality is for those who have found God in the midst of hell. Authentic Christian spirituality embraces the perpetual perishing of life, the pain of separation and guilt, and the anguish of bereavement and death as well as the joy of childbirth, the ecstasy of young love, and the radical wonder of the divine-human partnership.

Spiritual transformation involves the reclaiming of the "basic trust" in the universe that many of us lost, or never found, in childhood. Confident that nothing can separate us from the love of God, we can discern blessings and growth even at life's descending edges.

What feelings come over you when you read the psalmist's affirmation of faith? "Even though I walk through the darkest valley, I fear no evil; for you are with me; your rod and your staff—they comfort me." What enemies are vanquished when you hear the Psalm's words of promise? "You prepare a table before me in the presence of my enemies; you anoint my head with oil; my cup overflows."

God is the "fellow sufferer who understands," but more than that, God is also the divine companion who guards us from evil. Although divine protection does not ensure absolute safety from harm, it does ensure ultimate security, for "I shall dwell in the house of the Lord my whole life long," regardless of the threats that assail me. Invoked in the context of threats against the saint's life, "St. Patrick's Breastplate" witnesses to a protection that embraces us wherever we go.

> I gird myself today with the power of God:
> God's strength to comfort me,
> God's might to uphold me,
> God's wisdom to guide me,
> God's eye to look before me,
> God's ear to hear me,
> God's word to speak for me,
> God's hand to lead me,
> God's way to lie before me,
> God's shield to protect me,
> God's angels to save me

From the snares of the Devil,
From temptations to sin,
From all who wish me ill…

May Christ guard me today,
From poison and fire,
From drowning and wounding,
So my mission may bear
Fruit in abundance.
Christ behind and before me,
Christ beneath and above me,
Christ with me and in me,
Christ around and about me,
Christ on my left and my right,
Christ when I rise in the morning,
Christ when I lie down at night,
Christ in each heart that thinks of me,
Christ in each mouth that speaks of me,
Christ in each eye that sees me,
Christ in each ear that hears me.

Surrounded as we are by God's presence, every place is home. We can find anointing and abundance amid controversy, persecution, and pain, for Christ's healing light permeates even the darkness of grief, death, and hell. When we cry out, there is one who listens; when we reach out, there is a guiding hand.

Precious Lord, take my hand, lead me on, let me stand,
I am tired, I am weak, I am worn;
through the storm, through the night, lead me on to the light:
Take my hand, precious Lord, lead me home.

When my way grows drear, precious Lord, linger near,
when my life is almost gone,
hear my cry, hear my call, hold my hand, lest I fall:
Take my hand, precious Lord, lead me home.

When the darkness appears and the night draws near,
and the day is past and gone,
at the river I stand, guide my feet, hold my hand:
Take my hand, precious Lord, lead me home.

THOMAS A. DORSEY, "PRECIOUS LORD, TAKE MY HAND"

EXERCISE ONE: LIVING BY YOUR AFFIRMATIONS

For your affirmation, simply repeat throughout the day, "God is with me in the darkest valley." Remember that even though you may not feel threatened at this time, all fears and anxieties point to the ultimate horizon of death and God-forsakenness. In living by Psalm 23, we affirm that our whole life finds its security in God's faithful care.

I have personalized this affirmation in the following fashion: "God is with me in *my fears about the future.*" "God is with me as *I worry about my father's well-being.*" "God is with me as *I face the challenges of the job search.*" How would you personalize this affirmation? What is the dark valley in your life?

God is with me in _____.
God is with me in _____.
God is with me as _____.
God is with me as _____.

EXERCISE TWO: LIVING BY YOUR IMAGINATION

In the quiet, take time to reflect on Psalm 23. What images are powerful to you today? What are the names of your fears, darknesses, and enemies?

In the quiet, imagine yourself walking through a lovely green valley. What things do you notice? What wonders capture your eyes? As you walk along, the beautiful valley gradually becomes more ominous as the light of day fades. As darkness envelops you, the sounds of the night surround you. What sounds do you hear? What predators lurk in the darkness? In the valley of your life, what darkness of mind, body, spirit, relationship, or external event threatens you? What enemies lurk in the shadows? How are you responding to these enemies today?

In the darkness you discover that you are not alone. Christ is with you, guiding and guarding you. His presence is a guiding light illuminating your path and dispersing your enemies.

How does it feel to have Christ as your companion?

In the midst of the darkness you come to a meadow, where Christ bids you to rest. Christ sets his heavenly feast for you. What good foods are prepared for you? "Taste and see the goodness of God." After the feast Christ anoints you with oil. What does it feel like to be anointed? How does your life change?

After you are rested you and Christ journey forth to your spiritual resting place. Take time to thank Christ for his protection and care.

EXERCISE THREE: FAITH IN ACTION

Many people are living in the valley of the shadow of death. In nursing homes and hospices, many persons are preparing for the final journey. Medical studies note that physicians and nurses tend to avoid dying persons. Take time to reflect on your feelings about death. Take time to reflect on the uneasiness you may experience around dying persons. Ask God for the strength to face your fears of death and dying. If you feel the call, you may consider becoming a volunteer at a hospice, where the focus of care is on the spiritual, emotional, relational, and pain-relief needs of dying persons rather than the prolongation of life.

I Am Rising with Christ

> *[Christ] was raised on the third day in accordance with*
> *the scriptures...."Death has been swallowed up in victory."*
> *"Where, O death, is your victory? Where, O death, is*
> *your sting?" The sting of death is sin, and the power of*
> *sin is the law. But thanks be to God, who gives us the*
> *victory through our Lord Jesus Christ.*
>
> 1 CORINTHIANS 15:4, 54b–57

The heart of the Christian story is the dynamic interplay of crucifixion and resurrection.

For the apostle Paul and the early Christians, the cross and resurrection were both personal and cosmic events. Through the power of God, Jesus of Nazareth, the one who died in agony and abandonment, was raised from the dead as a sign of God's universal aim at new life in the midst of death. Although scholars debate the factuality of Jesus' resurrection, it is clear that the resurrection of Jesus was a living reality from the very beginning of Christian experience. It is a living reality today for countless Christians.

The nature of the resurrection is a mystery transcending the limitations of narrow empirical reasoning. The spiritual body of Christ goes beyond, yet includes, the realities of physical existence. It cannot be encompassed by the literalistic reasoning of fundamentalist Christians or the rationalist limitations of biblical scholars. But it is experienced when new life emerges in the valley of the shadow of death.

Christ is risen! Christ is risen indeed in the transformation of the first-century disciples and the apostle Paul. The risen Christ is still alive wherever the forces of life overcome the powers of death and evil. In every time and place, the spirit of resurrection addresses humankind, inviting people to choose life and giving them the power to become "new creations." The resurrection comes to us as a power and a possibility whose origin is beyond ourselves and our own efforts. But it is also the power actively working within our quests for abundant and transformed lives. God has rolled away the stone and the future is alive, but we must choose, with Lazarus, to come forth and embody the resurrection spirit that has been offered to us.

In the gospel of John's narrative of the resurrection, Mary Magdalene wanders grief-stricken into the garden. Even the angels cannot console her, for she needs the "real presence" of the risen Christ. She is raised to new life only when the risen Christ calls her by name in a voice that speaks from heart to heart. And so it is with ourselves, for we also need the "real presence" of the risen Christ. In darkest nights of fear, grief, and death, we are raised when the voice of the cosmic Christ, rising in all things, speaks with intimacy that only we can hear. Always a mystery, always beyond expectation, the spirit of resurrection comes to us with poetry, song, and surprise. Along with the poet e. e. cummings, all we can say is thank you, and with the hymn writer Charles Wesley, all we can say—and it is more than enough—is Alleluia!

> i thank You God for most this amazing
> day: for the leaping greenly spirits of trees
> and a blue true dream of sky, and for everything
> which is natural which is infinite which is yes
>
> (i who have died am alive again
> and this is the son's birthday: this is the birth
> day of life and love and wings: and of the gay
> great happening illimitably earth)...
>
> (now the ears of my ears awake and
> now the eyes of my eyes are opened)

Awakened to the resurrection, death loses its sting, and, unshackled by fear, we soar into God's realm of adventure and possibility.

> Christ the Lord is risen today, Alleluia!
> All creation join to say, Alleluia!
> Raise your joys and triumphs high, Alleluia!
> Sing, O heavens, and earth reply, Alleluia!
>
> Lives again our glorious King, Alleluia!
> Where, O death, is now your sting? Alleluia!
> Jesus died, our souls to save, Alleluia!
> Where your victory, O grave? Alleluia!
>
> Love's redeeming work is done, Alleluia!
> Fought the fight, the battle won, Alleluia!
> Death in vain forbids him rise, Alleluia!
> Christ has opened paradise. Alleluia!
>
> Soar we now where Christ has led, Alleluia!
> Following our exalted Head, Alleluia!

Made like him, like him we rise, Alleluia!
Ours the cross, the grave, the skies, Alleluia!

CHARLES WESLEY, "CHRIST THE LORD IS RISEN TODAY"

EXERCISE ONE: LIVING BY YOUR AFFIRMATIONS

As you ponder the reality of the resurrection in your life, affirm the resurrection truth: "I am rising with Christ." In my own life, I have embodied these affirmations in the following ways: "I am rising with Christ as *I choose new behaviors.*" "I am rising in Christ as *I face my fears of the death of myself and my father.*" "I am rising with Christ as *I overcome the limitations I have placed on myself.*" How would you embody the resurrection in your life?

I am rising with Christ as _____.
I am rising with Christ as _____.
I am rising with Christ as _____.
I am rising with Christ as _____.

EXERCISE TWO: LIVING BY YOUR IMAGINATION

In your experience of the resurrection, I invite you to live the adventure of Mary Magdalene. Take some time to be still. Read the resurrection story found in John 20:1–18. Let the words and images sink in.

It is the darkest of days. Your dear friend Jesus has just died a painful and humiliating death. Your heart is broken as you go to pay your final respects to your teacher and friend.

How are you feeling as you walk to the tomb? When you discover that the tomb is empty, how do you feel? What losses do you feel today? What has died and is lost in your own life?

As you wander the garden, you discover that you are not alone. A mysterious figure stands beside you and calls you by name. Hear your name spoken in the silence of the garden. How does it feel for this mysterious figure to call you by name? You realize that the voice is familiar. It is the voice of Jesus, the healer, teacher, and friend. How does it feel to have Jesus, the risen One, call your name? What do you want to share with Jesus? What does he say to you about the meaning of the resurrection in your life?

The time has come for you to leave the garden. Jesus takes your hand and speaks your name again, " _____, I will be with you always. _____, you are rising triumphantly with me from now on."

Exercise Three: Faith in Action

An essential part of the resurrection experience is the proclamation of the good news: "Christ is risen...I have seen the Lord." In a world often dominated by death, choose this day to live by the resurrection. Ask God to guide you to persons and situations in which the powers of death threaten to destroy life—aging and dying, addiction, homelessness, hate crimes.

Although there is no one response that is appropriate, open yourself to live out the resurrection in the death-full situations of life. Become, by your words and actions, a witness to the resurrection in your family, church, and community.

I Thank You, God, for the Wonder
of My Being

Rejoice always, pray without ceasing, give thanks in all circumstances; for this is the will of God in Christ Jesus for you.

1 THESSALONIANS 5:16–18

At the heart of process-relational spirituality is the experience of gratitude. The affirmations of faith are grounded in the abundance of the universe and in the constantly unfolding potentials for divine transformation in each moment of life. German mystic Meister Eckhardt once asserted, "If the only prayer you can make is thank you, that will be enough."

Gratitude awakens us to a sense of wonder, adventure, innovation, and creativity. Our prayers of thanksgiving remind us even in the most difficult of settings that God is working for good and that God will supply our deepest needs. To be thankful is to say yes to life and to live by what Rabbi Abraham Heschel described as "radical amazement." In moments of thanksgiving, we glimpse the intricately woven strands of divine providence that manifest themselves in synchronous encounters, bursts of unexpected energy, and life-changing insights. God constantly makes a way where there is no way in the deliverance of individuals and communities. Divine providence shapes our journeys and invites us to become cocreators each moment and over a lifetime as we blend our creativity with our neighbors and the One within whom we live, move, and have our being.

> Now thank we all our God with heart and hands and voices,
> who wondrous things has done, in whom the world rejoices,
> who, from our mothers' arms, has blessed us on our way
> with countless gifts of love, and still is ours today.
>
> O may this bounteous God through all our life be near us
> with ever joyful hearts and blessed peace to cheer us,
> and keep us full of grace, and guide us when perplexed,
> and free us from all ills in this world and the next.
>
> MARTIN RINKART, "NOW THANK WE ALL OUR GOD."

In our affirmations of faith, the personal and the communal aspects of providence are joined. The heavens above and the cells of our bodies declare God's intimate care. Abundant life is ours as we open to the divine energy and gratefully share it with everyone. With thankful hearts, scarcity becomes abundance and isolation becomes community. All we can say in all the seasons of life is thank you.

> I thank you, Jesus, thank you, Jesus,
> thank you, Jesus, my Savior God,
> for you brought me, yes, you brought me
> from a mighty, a mighty long way...
>
> You've been my father, been my mother,
> been my sister, my brother, too,
> for you brought me, yes, you brought me
> from a mighty, a mighty long way.
>
> KENNETH MORRIS, "I THANK YOU, JESUS"

EXERCISE ONE: LIVING BY YOUR AFFIRMATIONS

Today, simply take time to affirm your gratitude to God: "I thank you God for the wonder of my being," or "I thank you God for the wonder of all being." This affirmation, which I initially learned at the Shalem Institute for Spiritual Formation in Washington, D.C., can be personalized in an infinite number of ways. In my life, I affirm my gratitude in the following ways: "I thank you God for the wonder of *my creativity*." "I thank you God for the wonder of *Matt's being*." "I thank you God for *the beauty of the morning*." How would you personalize this?

I thank you God for the wonder of _____.
I thank you God for the wonder of _____.
I thank you God for the wonder of _____.
I thank you God for the wonder of _____.

EXERCISE TWO: LIVING BY YOUR IMAGINATION

In the quiet, take time to "count your blessings." Visualize each of your gifts and blessings. Take time to thank God for the many gifts you have received. Look at a challenge in your life. Take time to open yourself to God's movement even in this difficult situation. Thank God for the divine care that constantly sustains us, especially in difficult situations.

As I stated earlier, imaginative prayer can be integrated into your daily exercise routine. Many persons regularly practice "walking prayer." Whether you walk quickly or at a deliberate meditative pace, your walk can be a time for spiritual growth. Often, I take time in the quiet of a walk to visualize and then thank God for the gifts of my life—vocation, relationships, family, parental love, opportunities, and so forth. I have seldom run out of things and persons for which to be thankful. In this regular commitment to mindful thanksgiving, I have found a new appreciation for the wonders of the earth, relationships, and my own life. I have found that I can "taste and see" the goodness of God, even in the most unlikely situations.

EXERCISE THREE: FAITH IN ACTION

In the spirit of the affirmations of faith, commit yourself to be a channel of gratitude. Take time to express your thanks for the many interactions in the course of a day. As you look at the world with the abundant eyes of gratitude and the generosity of thanksgiving, your world will be transformed, as will be the people that you encounter. Take time to express your thanks for the smallest of gifts—a smile or a kind word, a spouse's preparation of the morning coffee, a colleague's e-mail, a friend's phone call, a waiter's service. In your daily life, look for the light, not the darkness; notice the abundance, not the scarcity. "Rejoice always, pray without ceasing, give thanks in all circumstances, for God eternally loves you and will supply your deepest needs"—these are the affirmations of faith.

A FINAL WORD

Living by your affirmations is a lifelong adventure. After you have completed this book, you may choose to continue the adventure of spiritual transformation. Indeed, the adventure will happen whether or not you consciously choose it. As you seek to embody the affirmative spirituality of this book, you may wish to focus specifically on certain affirmations of faith or visualization exercises found within the text. In my own journey, I have been nurtured by affirmations such as: "My God shall supply my every need." "God is with me." "Nothing shall separate me from the love of God." I have also regularly lived with the spiritual practices of centering prayer, breath prayer, and visualizations involving divine healing.

In the weeks ahead, you may feel called to initiate a spiritual formation group in your church or with friends from various spiritual communities, using this book or one of the many excellent group spirituality texts available today.

Remember that God is always with you in your journey and that you are in a holy adventure in companionship and cocreation with a dynamic and living God. Thanks be to God for the wonder of all being.

Notes

CHAPTER ONE

[1]Victor Frankl, *From Death Camp to Existentialism* (Boston: Beacon Press, 1959), 65.

[2]Ibid., 72.

[3]Ibid., 74.

[4]Ibid., 75.

[5]Martin Luther King, Jr., *Strength to Love* (Philadelphia: Fortress Press, 1963), 113–14.

[6]Harold Koenig, *The Healing Power of Faith* (New York: Simon & Schuster, 1999), 24–25.

[7]Dale Matthews, *The Faith Factor* (New York: Viking, 1998).

[8]Agnes Sanford, *The Healing Light* (St. Paul: Macalester Park, 1972), 28–29.

[9]Ibid., 44.

[10]Ruth Carter Stapleton, *The Gift of Inner Healing* (Waco: Word Books, 1976); Dennis and Matthew Linn, *Healing Life's Hurts* (New York: Paulist Press, 1978).

CHAPTER TWO

[1]Alfred North Whitehead, *Process and Reality* (New York: Free Press, 1978), 346.

[2]Ibid., 351.

[3]*Poems of Gerard Manley Hopkins*, 3d ed., ed. W. H. Gardner (Oxford: Oxford University Press, 1948).

CHAPTER FOUR

[1]King, *Strength to Love,* 7.

[2]Ibid., 8.

CHAPTER FIVE

[1]For a more extensive theological and spiritual reflection on the nature of death and dying, see Bruce Epperly, *At the Edges of Life* (St. Louis: Chalice Press, 1992).

[2]For a more detailed understanding of the healing ministry of Jesus, I refer you to Morton Kelsey, *Psychology, Medicine, and Christian Healing* (New York: Harper and Row, 1988).